HANDMADE
TILES

HANDMADE
TILES

DESIGNING ◆ MAKING ◆ DECORATING

FRANK GIORGINI

David & Charles

A DAVID & CHARLES BOOK

First published in the United States of America by Lark Books

Copyright © Frank Giorgini 1994

UK edition first published 1995

Frank Giorgini has asserted his right to be identified as author of this work in accordance with the Copyright, Designs and Patents Act 1988.

A catalogue record for this book is available from the British Library.

ISBN 0 7153 0338 4

Typeset by Greenshires Icon, Exeter
and printed in Singapore by C. S. Graphics Ltd
for David & Charles
Brunel House Newton Abbot Devon

CONTENTS

INTRODUCTION

What is it about ceramic tiles that is so alluring and so comforting? For some people, it may be their permanence. Tiles have existed since the times of the Roman Empire and the Babylonians. For others, the sight of a tile may recall wonderful childhood memories of standing in a warm kitchen or lying in a steaming bath. Tiles certainly tend to linger, not just in our memories but in actual space as well. Unlike wallpaper or paint, they aren't replaced frequently. The shapes and images that are frozen in time on their surfaces can create an environment that affects generations to come.

Whatever their charm for individuals, the appeal of tiles spans the globe. Every culture with the technology and resources to do so has produced ceramic tiles. The levels of technology vary, of course, from hand-dug clay slabs, dried in the sun and fired with old car tyres, to colossal factories hydraulically dust-pressing thousands of tiles per hour around the clock.

Clay has been my preferred medium in artistic expression for over twenty years. Although it's relatively valueless in its raw state, clay can be transformed by the human hand into objects of enduring beauty. And the process of shaping it is wonderfully practical and direct. This abundant material, so inviting to the touch, is completely malleable. It has no grain or direction and can be squeezed, pushed, scraped, paddled and moulded into almost any imaginable shape – from utilitarian vessels to sculptural objects and from decorative surfaces to musical instruments.

There is something very satisfying about working with clay. As you shape it, you 'touch the earth'. Through the miracle of hand, heart and mind, you literally make something from nothing. My students at Parsons School of Design, where I've taught ceramic tile design and fabrication courses since 1985, include matriculated undergraduates in art and design, professionals in other disciplines of the art field, and people with no previous experience in art or clay. All of them, however, enjoy being able to express themselves with this user-friendly material. When they make a mistake, they just wad the clay back up and start again.

You don't need an art background to make tiles. In fact, some of the most exciting tiles in my classes come from students without one. People who get caught up in trying to make a tile that is 'good art' often produce work that is contrived and lacking in vitality. If you can open up, instead, and express yourself from within, you will probably do very well.

My purpose in this book is to provide you with the techniques necessary to transform your images and ideas into the ceramic tile format. Once you've been introduced to the history of handmade tiles (in Chapter 1, written by Joseph Taylor of the Tile Heritage Foundation), you'll find that the chapter arrangement is based on the stages of the tile-making process. Descriptions of kilns, raw clay, tools and studio space come first. Subsequent chapters extend from the process of shaping moist, malleable clay, fresh out of the bag, all the way to installing your finished work. Making relief tiles, decorating both unfired and biscuit-fired clay, and firing your tiles, are all explained in detail. In addition, I've included chapters on mosaics, tile design, and health and safety, and – for readers who are handy in the workshop – instructions for making your own tools, including a studio tile press.

I address many methods of surface decoration, but my forte is the sculpting and handforming of clay tiles, and my emphasis is on the actual process of handmaking tiles. The step-by-step process for making relief tiles from plaster press moulds is one of the tile-making methods that this book covers in detail. Transforming an amorphous lump of earthen material into a three-dimensional representation of my concept and vision is my idea of a good time.

Because I'm used to working with students whose experience and skill levels range from expert to nonexistent, I've tried to use the same teaching methods here – and to cover the same techniques – as I do in my classroom. It's therefore my hope that this book will be both a practical introduction for the novice and a valuable resource for the professional ceramist.

CHAPTER ONE

A HISTORY OF
TILE MAKING

Opposite page:
Bernadette Stillo
Celebrate Life.
1993
5³/₄x7³/₄in
(14.6x19.7cm)
PHOTOGRAPH BY BOBBY
HANSSON

Tile depicting
Vernal Falls in
Yosemite National
Park. Claycraft
Potteries,
Los Angeles,
California,
c.1926.
Tile Heritage
Foundation.
Gift of Bart
Huffman.

Sixteenth-century 'cuenca' tiles. From the Museo Nacional de Cerámica Gonzalez Marti, Valencia, Spain. © Instituto de Promoción Cerámica, Castellón, Spain.
PHOTOGRAPH BY JORGE CRESPO

Late fourteenth-century tile work in the Alhambra (Granada, Spain). Patio de los Arrayanes. © Instituto de Promoción Cerámica, Castellón, Spain.
PHOTOGRAPH BY ALGARA/GARRIDO

THE HANDCRAFTED TRADITION IN CERAMIC TILES

BY JOSEPH A. TAYLOR

Today ceramic tiles are, more often than not, regarded as functional objects. We use them in our kitchens and bathrooms, on floors throughout our homes, for very practical reasons: their durability and ease of maintenance. Characterized by size, shape, colour and design, tiles possess a particular beauty which, although a consideration, is often of secondary importance. Historically, however, this has not always been the case. Although the function of a tile has been significant, aesthetics have also played a major role.

From excavations in various parts of the world, archaeologists are continuing to find bits and pieces of both pottery and tiles dating back thousands of years. Just how long fired tiles have actually been produced or just where the first tiles were installed are questions that may never be answered. Throughout the history of civilization, however, there have been periods when tiles have emerged and flourished primarily as a decorative medium, influenced by social, political and economic forces as well as by the technology at hand.

Numerous palaces and public buildings of the ancient world were adorned with decorative tiles, including the Assyrian Palace of Sargon at Khorsabad (722–705 BC), the imposing Ishtar Gate built by Nebuchadnezzar II in Babylon (604–562 BC) and the palaces of King Darius at Susa and Persepolis in ancient Persia (521–486 BC). Considerably earlier, small brightly coloured blue tiles were used to decorate the interior of the tomb of King Zoser of Egypt (2630–2611 BC) in the stepped pyramid at Sakkara.

Through the millenniums numerous factors influenced the development and proliferation of decorative tiles. Movement along major trade routes, both on land and by sea, encouraged the exchange of ideas and materials especially where these routes intersected. Similarly wars, political unrest and religious fervour all played a part in the blending of cultures and the subsequent artistic output in any given part of the world. When the Islamic warriors, for example, overran the territories of the Near and Middle East in the seventh century, the leaders were irresistibly attracted to the artistic accomplishments of the peoples they conquered. They developed a keen appreciation for the locals' sense of colour and design which they carried with them into Turkey, across North Africa and eventually into Spain.

Although a myriad of architectural masterpieces have been lost, or relegated (in part) to museums for safe keeping, many examples of magnificent tilework still exist *in situ* throughout the world. Some of the most breathtaking in both colour and design are located in present-day Iran, such as the Royal Palace of Shah Addas I (1587–1628) in Isfahan as well as the spectacular mosques and mausoleums in that city. The Blue Mosque in Istanbul, built for Sultan Ahmet I between 1609 and 1616, is also particularly striking. This high degree of ceramic splendour has yet to be surpassed.

From ancient times, skilled craftsmen – both tile makers and installers – were respected members of society. Artisans were employed by the ruling governments and would travel to the centres of commerce and wealth to practise their skills. Over time there was an evolution of technique away from the laborious mosaic work of the early Persian craftsmen, who skilfully broke up pieces of glazed tile into standardized symbolic shapes to create a larger design. Various techniques greatly simplified the process while maintaining a similar aesthetic effect. For example, a linear pattern was painted onto the surface of a tile with a substance designed to resist the application of glaze. As the glazes were applied, the line served as a bar-

Spectacular tiles decorate the interior of the Blue Mosque in Istanbul. Courtesy of Kalebodur Seramik Sanayi A.S.

Sixteenth-century tiles create an arched effect over the interior windows of the Ramazan Efendi Mosque in Istanbul. Design is typical of Ottoman tile art at its height. Courtesy of Kalebodur Seramik Sanayi A.S.

Detail of tile panel between windows in Ramazan Efendi Mosque, Istanbul. Courtesy of Kalebodur Seramik Sanayi A.S.

One of a set of four Portuguese tile panels from the Convent of St Francis, Angra do Heroismo, Terceira, the Azores, depicting the parable of the Prodigal Son. Tin-glazed technique, artist unknown, early eighteenth century. Courtesy of Jim Green.

Clay tiles, dating from the twelfth century, cut in geometric shapes and arranged in patterns on the floor of the High Altar, Fountains Abbey, North Yorkshire, England.

rier between the colours. Originally developed in Persia, this technique is also in evidence throughout the Alhambra in Granada, Spain, the fortress built by the Moors in the latter half of the fourteenth century.

The introduction of Chinese porcelains into Persia and the West during the Tang Dynasty (618–906 AD) had far-reaching effects as artisans endeavoured for centuries thereafter to reproduce this exotic ware from local materials. The Persians developed a white tin-based slip to mask their red clays; brightly coloured designs could then be successfully applied to the white surface. Revived by the tile makers in Spain in the eleventh century, tin-glazed ware was called *maiolica* by the Italians as it came to them via the island of Majorca. The Dutch craftsmen developed their own version in the early sixteenth century, which later became known as *Delft* after one of the towns in Holland where the tiles were made. Many of these blue and white tiles depicted the fashions, games, myths and stories popular at the time.

During the twelfth century, handcrafted tiles with incised or raised designs, often in a variety of shapes and sizes, were made at Christian monasteries to decorate the floors of churches and abbeys throughout western Europe and the British Isles. The tiles were crude and earthy in appearance, either glazed in darker tones or left unglazed, and were frequently arranged in geometric patterns not unlike the earlier Roman mosaic floors from which they were probably derived. Inlaid tiles soon followed, where the design pressed into the tile was filled with a contrasting clay colour.

By the middle of the seventeenth century tile making in Europe had become a fully-fledged commercial enterprise, spurred on by a growing population, an evolving middle class and international trade. An increased awareness of the value of sanitized surfaces meant that tiles were being used with greater frequency and imagination in the home. They were also being exported from every country that made them, and the artisans were moving more freely about the Continent, adapting their skills to local materials and customs. The Dutch East India Company and other international traders were transporting tiles to the colonies and to other parts of the world, frequently using them as ballast on ships leaving Europe.

When the Europeans first arrived on the North American continent, there was no evidence of a tile making tradition. In the north-east and along the eastern seaboard, especially in the emerging metropolitan areas, many of the immigrants who built homes continued to look to England and the Continent for their tiles. As a result, tile importing companies were established in all of the major coastal cities. As was the custom in Britain and Europe, tiles were commonly used to decorate mantelpieces and hearths. By the 1850s, geometric arrangements of unglazed tiles in various colours became the preferred floor covering for domestic and commercial entrances.

Emerging from the period of reconstruction following the American Civil War, people in the United States could focus more on domestic matters. A reflection of one's good taste and social status, decorative tiles were considered a virtual necessity in any fashionable home. A major turning point occured in 1876 with the Centennial Exposition in Philadelphia where European and British manufacturers put on an impressive display of both pottery and tiles. From that time onward, American craftsmen and entrepreneurs embraced the challenge, and North American tile production took hold.

The first decorative tiles produced in the United States were called 'art tiles', and they reflected the aesthetics and manufacturing methods prevalent in the British Isles and on the Continent. Produced primarily as ornamentation,

Two 'art' tiles, c.1880, designed for use on a fireplace mantel.
Chelsea Keramic Art Works, Chelsea, Massachusetts. Private collection.

these were for the most part relief tiles, frequently depicting scenes from nature or classical motifs. They were produced from clay dust in bulky screw presses and coloured in glossy, translucent glazes over a white clay body. The machinery used in making these early tiles was rudimentary; a great deal of handwork was involved. The presses were manually operated and much of the finishing work and glazing was done by hand. Most notably, each decorative tile had to be initially modelled in clay by an experienced artist-craftsman before it went into production.

An early centre of tile making was Chelsea, Massachusetts, just north of Boston, where members of the Robertson family from Scotland gathered in the late 1860s and established the Chelsea Keramic Art Works. John Gardner Low (1835–1907) was apprenticed at the Art Works and in 1877, prompted by his father's financial backing, founded the J. & J.G. Low Art Tile Works, which produced award-winning tiles known for their innovative designs. His 'natural process' tiles, for example, were made by pressing grasses, leaves and other organic matter into the soft clay surface before firing.

Zanesville, Ohio, also became a major site for tile manufacture. In 1876 the American Encaustic Tiling Company started producing unglazed geometric floor tiles. Over its nearly 60 years of operation, the company produced virtually every type of tile imaginable and grew to be the largest tile company in the world. In 1887 the company hired Herman Mueller (1854–1941), a German-born artist-sculptor. He expanded the product line to include art tiles of the highest quality. In 1894, together with chemist Karl Langenbeck, Mueller formed Mosaic Tile, also in Zanesville, a company which would soon become another giant of the industry.

The emergence of handcrafted decorative tiles in the United States, beginning in the late 1890s, represented a rebellion against the conventional aesthetics of the Victorian era when tiles were viewed as mere ornaments, symbols of refined taste. The commercialization of both the product and the process, together with the impersonalization of the workplace, left little room for the artist or craftsman. Although tiles were becoming less expensive and more commonly used, most were mass-produced and lacked aesthetic appeal.

By the turn of the twentieth century, partially inspired by the Arts and Crafts Movement in England, there was a growing appreciation of individual craftsmanship in America. Rather than being manufactured as ornamental objects to serve some useful purpose once installed, individual tiles became an artistic medium, a means of self-expression for the craftsman. Subject matter was simplified: glossy, translucent glazes were replaced with matt finishes. The way a tile was produced became an essential part of its appearance: the handcrafted qualities were clearly visible and intentional.

Henry Chapman Mercer (1856–1930) was instrumental in bringing about these substantive changes, in redirecting what had been primarily a functional focus to become an artistic one, and his influence was so pervasive as to stretch from coast to coast. Initially established in small outbuildings in Doylestown, Pennsylvania, he named his enterprise the Moravian Pottery and Tile Works after the German-born stoveplate makers – some of his earliest tiles were developed from stoveplate designs.

Far from a manufacturing facility, Mercer's tile works was more of an artisan's studio where each tile was individually modelled by hand, from which a plaster mould would be made. Multiple tiles were then produced by hand-pressing soft clay into the mould. Mercer's designs were simple and straightforward, often based on historic subjects dating back to medieval times. Although he pro-

The J. & J.G. Low Art Tile Works of Chelsea, Massachusetts, was known for its innovative tile designs. Any one of these would have been used as an accent on either corner of a fireplace opening. C.1880. Private collection.

duced tiles for domestic use, especially for fireplace surrounds, he was also involved in a number of large commercial projects. One of these was the State Capitol in Harrisburg, Pennsylvania, for which he provided thousands of square feet of handcrafted floor tiles.

Other tile makers, contemporaries of Mercer's, also espoused Arts and Crafts principles and were strongly influenced by the tile maker from Doylestown. Among the most well known was William Grueby (1867–1925), a tile pioneer from Boston, who was apprenticed at the Low Art Tile Works before forming the Grueby Faience Company in 1894. By the turn of the century his matt green glaze was emulated by many of the established potteries.

The Rookwood Pottery, founded in Cincinnati, Ohio, by Maria Longworth Nichols in 1880, began producing tile and other architectural products in 1902. Noted for its high relief and waxy matt glaze treatments, the Rookwood tile found its way into numerous prestigious installations, both in commercial buildings and in upmarket private homes.

In 1903 Mary Chase Perry (1867–1961) teamed up with Horace Caulkins and founded the Pewabic Pottery in Detroit, named after the Pewabic Mine in Hancock, Michigan, where she was born. Both pottery and tiles were produced at Pewabic from the beginning. Akin to Mercer's in many ways, the tiles clearly and intentionally demonstrated the creativity of the artist. Perry became most well known for her glazes, specifically her iridescent blues and purples, and she was commissioned by respected architects for many commercial jobs, both in and outside Detroit.

The popularity of machine-made art tiles had diminished by the turn of the century and had all but disappeared by 1910. By this time handcrafted tiles, or those made by machine to appear handmade, dominated the market. Throughout the 1910s and 1920s, tiles were used with increasing imagination to decorate the walls and floors of various rooms in the home, and even the patios, walkways and gardens outside. Tiles in contrasting colours and in varying shapes and sizes were used in the same

installation, often with striking results. Bright colours and geometric patterns were particularly popular throughout the southern and western American states. By the mid-1920s, ceramic tiles were in many areas more than a symbol of good taste; they had become an integral part of most new homes.

The production of decorative tiles in California lagged behind the rest of the United States, primarily because adequate quantities of tiles were available from the eastern manufacturers to meet the demand. However, the population began to mushroom in the major urban areas following the turn of the century. Although some tiles were made there as early as 1900, it was another ten years before a unique tile-making tradition was established in the state.

Ernest Batchelder (1875–1957), born and educated in the east of the United States, abandoned a successful teaching career in 1910 and began making tiles in his backyard in Pasadena. Clearly inspired by Mercer's Moravian tiles, Batchelder hand-pressed his tiles from plaster moulds and coloured them with clay slips rather than glazes. He integrated the clay body into the overall aesthetic of each tile by partially rubbing off the colouring agent, exposing the clay underneath, and thus leaving a mottled effect on the surface. Like Mercer, Batchelder was drawn to medieval imagery, yet many of his tiles include features of the Californian landscape as well.

By 1920 Batchelder had outgrown his small factory in Pasadena, and he moved to a much larger one just north of downtown Los Angeles, where he employed up to 175 people at the height of his production in the mid-1920s. He exhibited his tiles in most of the major cities in the United States.

The earthy, handcrafted appearance of Batchelder's tiles had broad appeal, and this type of low-relief design attracted the attention of a handful of other talented ceramists who wished to capitalize on his success. Among these was Fred Robertson (1869–1952), the grandson of the founder of the Chelsea Keramic Art Works two generations earlier,

This pair of classical figures, designed for either side of a fireplace opening, may well have been modelled by Herman Mueller for the American Encaustic Tiling Company of Zanesville, Ohio, c.1890. Private collection.

Christopher Columbus arriving on the North American shore. St Nicholas Church, Zanesville, Ohio, 1898. This mural exemplifies Herman Mueller's new system for producing encaustic tiles at the Mosaic Tile Company in Zanesville.

Top: Tile designed by Arthur Osborne for the J. & J.G. Low Art Tile Works of Chelsea, Massachusetts, c.1880. Note the mark in the lower right-hand corner, an encircled A. Private collection.

Second tile down: The 'natural process' tiles were among the most unusual produced by the J. & J.G. Low Art Tile Works of Chelsea, Massachusetts, c.1880. Private collection.

Two tiles immediately above: Portrait tiles designed for the two upper corners of a fireplace surround. Modelled by Isaac Broome for the Trent Tile Company, Trenton, New Jersey, c.1885. Private collection.

One of over four hundred pictorial mosaic panels designed for the floor of the Pennsylvania State Capitol in Harrisburg, 1903. Henry Chapman Mercer, Moravian Pottery and Tile Works, Doylestown, Pennsylvania.

who became the superintendent at Claycraft Potteries in Los Angeles in 1921. The manufacturing process and overall aesthetic of Claycraft tiles was similar to Batchelder's, but a unique feature of these tiles was the depiction in remarkable detail of specific landscapes from California.

Back in 1911, when Batchelder was grappling with clay in his backyard in Pasadena, a tile company of profound importance was getting under way in National City, just south of San Diego. California China Products Company was founded by Walter Nordhoff (1858–1937), a journalist-rancher turned entrepreneur, who was commissioned to provide the tiles for the Panama–California International Exposition that was to be held in Balboa Park in 1915. The bright colours and geometric patterns on the tiles, extraordinary in their brilliance and craftsmanship, were a perfect complement to the Spanish Colonial architecture, reflecting the romanticized traditions of Mexico and Spain. This type of tile became extremely popular throughout California, dominating both architecture and interior design for the next twenty years.

Rufus B. Keeler (1885–1934) was a major player in the manufacturing of decorative tiles in southern California. Having worked for a number of clay products companies in the state, Keeler started his own business in 1917, handcrafting tiles for fireplace surrounds. He greatly expanded his operation in 1923, forming the California Clay Products Company, which produced both the brightly coloured geometric designs and a glazed version of a press-moulded tile more in the style of Ernest Batchelder. In 1926 Keeler established the Malibu Potteries on the beach to the west of Los Angeles, and for the next six years he produced some of the most beautiful tiles of the pre-Depression period.

Among the handful of companies producing handcrafted tiles in northern California during this time were two of note, Solon & Schemmel and California Faience. The former was founded in 1920 by Albert Solon (1887–1949) from the prominent family of English ceramists. The latter, California Faience, was formed in Berkeley five years earlier by William Bragdon (1884–1959) and Chauncey Thomas (1877–1950), both accomplished ceramists from

the East. Among their many commissions, the most prestigious was the palatial mansion of William Randolph Hearst at San Simeon, designed by architect Julia Morgan and built during the 1920s. Wall surfaces, floors, patio inserts, stair risers, friezes, chimney tops and towers, all create a striking display of pattern and colour that enlivens the whole environment.

The Great Depression of the 1930s all but eliminated the tile industry in the United States, and the factories that survived were soon converted to support the war effort, which lasted well into the 1940s. After the war, tiles were in short supply, and factories were re-established to meet the unprecedented postwar demand. But times had changed; the flair of the 1920s and early 1930s had expired. Tiles were once again being mass produced, this time in pastel colours and in standard sizes with only minimal attention given to design. Handcrafted tiles had all but disappeared.

Following a lapse of nearly thirty years, the handcrafted tradition in tile making re-emerged during the 1960s, seemingly as an adjunct to contemporary pottery. There was a renewed focus on glaze treatments and surface textures, in earth tones and in the overall aesthetic of the tile. Tiles were promoted as architectural products and were used to clad the exterior of public buildings as well as the interiors of custom-built homes.

As the decade progressed, colour became a more dominant concern. There was a move away from earth tones in favour of lighter, more neutral glaze colours. By the early 1980s there evolved a preference for larger sizes and a cleaner, more pristine installation; imported tiles became particularly popular. Gradually, however, as the decade progressed, there was a renewed appreciation of individual craftsmanship and increasing numbers of handcrafted tiles appeared.

By 1990 a substantial market had been established. Most major cities had dealers specializing exclusively in high quality, handcrafted ware, and tiles were being promoted in the most imaginative ways. No longer reserved for the walls, floors and surfaces in kitchens and bathrooms, tiles had become a decorative art form in and of itself, its use limited only by one's imagination.

Part of one of the magnificent inlaid tile pavements designed by
A.W.N. Pugin for his 'gem', St. Giles Church, Cheadle, Staffordshire, c.1846.

Minton inlaid tile depicting a king
(probably Henry III), based on
a design in the Chapter House, Westminster
Abbey. The design dates from about
1842, but this example c.1850.
Private collection.

The handcrafted tradition in tile making, dating back to prehistoric times when man first recognized clay as a medium for artistic expression, is at present experiencing a renaissance the likes of which has not been previously seen. Literally hundreds of tile artists and artisans, muralists and mosaicists have emerged from their backyards and small studios across the country, and many of the larger manufacturers have refocused their production to include decorative lines. Today, there is no question: history is being made.

TILES IN BRITAIN

BY MICHAEL SPENDER

When Henry VIII's Dissolution of the Monasteries in the early sixteenth century caused the demand for architectural tiles to dwindle to a trickle, the zenith of medieval tile making was long past. Some 250 years had elapsed since the Chertsey tilers had created their figurative masterpieces and since the great pavement at Westminster Abbey Chapter House had been constructed. From this thirteenth-century high-point, when inlaid floor tiles were an integral element of the flowering of Gothic architecture and applied arts, the next two hundred years saw a steady decline in quality, off-set only by local revivals, notably at Great Malvern.

When volume tile making did re-commence in Britain, it was principally in the form of earthenware wall tiles. Following the accession of William and Mary to the English throne in 1689 the fashion for things Dutch led to an influx of potters from the Low Countries. By 1740 a distinctive tradition of decorative English tiles was emerging in centres such as Bristol and Liverpool. At first these tin-glazed tiles were painted in the Dutch manner, if rather more freely. But in the 1750s the Liverpool firm of Sadler and Green pioneered the use of transfer-printing from engravings onto tiles.

Transfer-printing speeded up the decorating process, but it was not until Herbert Minton (1793–1858) acquired Richard Prosser's 1840 patent for dust-pressing clay buttons, adapting it to mechanical tile-production, that the manufacturing process became one of mass-production.

Minton had worked for the family pottery from the 1820s and his taste for the Gothic Revival was reflected in an interest in medieval inlaid tiles. By 1842 he had successfully developed a process for manufacturing inlaid (or *encaustic* as they were known) tiles based on Samuel Wright's 1830 patent, of which he had bought a share. In later decades *encaustic* tiles were commonly dust-pressed, but the characteristic Minton process, using plastic clay inlaid with coloured slips, was labour-intensive and retained hand crafted quality.

By around 1842 Minton produced a series of tiles copying some of those in the thirteenth-century Westminster Abbey Chapter House pavement. His interest in Gothic forms was shared by the prolific architect and designer A.W.N. Pugin (1812–52), whom he is thought to have first met in 1840. Moving on from straight copies of medieval motifs, Pugin created for Minton strongly designed, often multi-coloured floor tiles that raised the ceramist's developing technical skills to new heights.

Other potteries, such as Chamberlain of Worcester and Godwin of Hereford made their own Gothic inlaid tiles. Some of these were excellent imitations of medieval examples, intended for the extensive church restoration of the time, such as that being carried out by Sir George Gilbert Scott (1811–78). They also worked with architects and designers such as William Burges (1827–81) and J.P. Seddon (1827–1906). But the profound creativity and inventiveness of Pugin's geometric and floral pattern-making was without equal. The last decade of Pugin's short life saw a collaboration with Minton that was to influence tile design, and more importantly the increased role of the designer in the manufacturing process, for the rest of tile history.

By 1849 Minton was using Collins and Reynolds' patented process for transfer printing from stone or metal 'blocks' onto dust-pressed wall tiles. Pugin immediately found the flat colour patterns possible with this process much more to his liking than the transfer of line engravings.

For the Medieval Court at the 1851 Great Exhibition in London, Pugin designed a set of embossed and pierced stove tiles, decorated with majolica glazes. Minton's art

Minton inlaid tile in four colours designed by A.W.N. Pugin, c.1850. This example is lit to show the three-dimensional effect of the recessed blue slip within the buff moulded design.

Moulded majolica-glazed tile in a geometric design reminiscent of the work of J.P. Seddon and Christopher Dresser. From a complex dado panel shown by Maw & Co. at the 1867 Paris Exhibition. Private collection.

director, Leon Arnoux (1816–1902) had developed this opaque, polychromatic glazing technique at the end of the 1840s, providing an alternative to the industry's usual thin, translucent glazes, and especially suitable to three-dimensional wares. In following decades thick majolica glazes were extensively and effectively used, notably at Minton and Maw, to give rich, colourful effects on often deeply moulded tile bodies.

Pugin's specially designed encaustic pavements graced not only his churches and cathedrals, but also the Palace of Westminster. Following his example English-made decorative tile schemes were over subsequent decades installed in buildings around the world, from Minton's floors in the Capitol, Washington, to Maw & Co's polychromatic decoration of the Victoria railway terminus in Bombay.

By the time of Pugin's death in 1852, at the age of forty, the manufacturing processes and the decorative techniques were established for the extraordinary tile boom of late Victorian Britain. In attaining this alongside Herbert Minton, Pugin was, as in so much of his work, ahead of his time, for the social and economic factors that combined to create the tile boom were not yet present.

The tile industry's rapid expansion from the 1860s into the 1870s marks the arrival of this boom. Enormous factories were established, with such resonant names as Minton China Works and Minton Hollins (a split of the earlier business), Copeland, Maw, Craven Dunnill. Other great ceramic companies partly built their late Victorian reputations on tile production, for example Wedgwood, Pilkington, Doulton. In 1879, near the peak of tile production, just one of these, Minton Hollins, was reputedly capable of churning out some eighteen million tiles each year!

Tiles were used everywhere, in the church and the museum, in the office and the factory, and, of course, all over the home. The late Victorian spate of house-building created an unprecedented demand for tiles. Geometric paving was used to enhance the hallway or the conservatory, but the real boom area was in decorated dust-pressed 'wall' tiles: in

the scullery, in the nursery, in the fireplace, on the washstand and latterly in the bathroom. And painted pictorial tile murals by firms such as Doulton and W.B. Simpson were erected in hospitals, shops and theatres across the land. A particularly well-known set of panels in Art Nouveau style was designed by Doulton's W.J. Neatby (1860–1910) for Harrod's and installed in the store's meat hall in 1902.

The insatiability of the tile market inevitably led to much debased commercial design work. Successful patterns were plagiarized or re-used by lesser manufacturers, often because the protection afforded by design registration had elapsed. Poorly copied Minton designs would resurface on unidentified blanks. (Conversely, it is often not registered who designed which tiles, and attribution regularly has to be made on stylistic grounds.)

Overall, artistic standards were upheld by the wide availability of figurative and abstract work by many of the leading designers and artists of late Victorian Britain. The popularity of illustrative transfer-printed tiles led to welldesigned, sometimes hand-coloured series by Walter Crane (1845–1915), Kate Greenaway (1846–1901), Thomas Allen (1831–1915), John Moyr Smith (fl. c.1872–89), William Wise (1847–89) and others. Wise's engraved copies of prints by the animal painter Robert Hills, and Smith's block-printed illustrations to Shakespeare, Tennyson and Walter Scott were immensely successful.

The Puginesque sense of strong design and pattern was however kept to the fore by the greatest designers of the period, including Christopher Dresser (1834–1904) and C.F.A. Voysey (1857–1941). These men in their different ways inherited the mantle of Pugin. Like him they applied their talents to a complete range of decorative and functional objects, including tiles. Voysey continued Pugin's ethos of quality craftsmanship into the twentieth century, in lyrical organic, moulded patterns.

Dresser bestrode late nineteenth-century design. He introduced muscular geometric styling to block-printed tiles for a mass market. His inspirational design sense and

Pair of majolica-glazed tiles from a fireplace surround by Maw & Co, c.1871. These moulded heads were singled out by the company as prime examples of modern majolica work. Private collection.

Viol, from a series of *Greek Musicians* designed by Thomas Allen for Wedgwood, c.1885. The male figure derives from a work by the painter Albert Moore. This dust-pressed tile is hand-painted over a line transfer-print. Private collection.

Chequered design of birds and foliage by William De Morgan, hand-painted in red lustre on a commercial blank. This tile probably dates from the 1870s, during De Morgan's Chelsea period. Private collection.

Vanity Fair, an eight-inch block-printed and hand-coloured tile from the *Pilgrim's Progress* series designed by John Moyr Smith as a freelance for Minton Hollins, c.1875. Private collection.

Sunday, from the nursery series *Days of the Week,* designed by Ellen E. Houghton for Minton China Works, c.1880. The design is transfer-printed and hand-coloured. Private collection.

Pair of Maw & Co tiles block-printed with classical designs by Walter Crane, c.1880. Private collection.

his fashionable use of Japanese patterns and motifs inspired a host of imitative designs. In an eclectic age, tile design was as much prey to worldwide influences as any of the applied arts. Cultural artefacts from all corners of the globe flooded into Imperial Britain and introduced an often confused myriad of exotic styles and motifs. Tile designers naturally gravitated towards countries with strong ceramic and tile traditions, like Persia, China and Spain.

In this age of mass-production the market for quality, individually made tiles fostered by Minton and Pugin never died. In 1871 Minton's Art Pottery Studio opened in Kensington Gore, producing individual painted tiles to designs by artists such as Henry Stacey Marks (1829–98) and E.J. Poynter (1836–1919), as well as generating ideas for the company's Stoke-on-Trent operations.

William Morris (1834–96) reacted against the commercial wares that abounded and from the 1860s was importing hand-made Dutch blanks for his workers to hand-decorate to his designs. Some beautiful panels were painted with figures and scenes by Edward Burne-Jones (1833–98).

William De Morgan (1839–1917) also worked for Morris & Co. and after 1870 started experimenting with lustre glazes inspired by Persian and Moorish tiles, using at first other companies' blanks and later his own, hand-fashioned plastic clay bodies. The iridescent lustre glazes were achieved by a reduction firing process which deposited a fine metallic film on the ceramic surface. De Morgan's fantastical beasts and repeating floral patterns are the epitome of the late nineteenth-century art tile. They inspired many arts and crafts makers as well as larger manufacturers. Pilkington developed its own 'Persian' patterns and glazes, some created by the Arts and Crafts designer Lewis F. Day (1845–1910), while Maw and Craven Dunnill capitalized on De Morgan's dazzling red lustre patterns.

Some makers, such as the Martin Brothers, made hand-crafted relief, incised or impressed tiles. But, exquisite as these are, in England these techniques did not perhaps attain the achievements of the Moravian Pottery, Grueby or Batchelder in the United States. The English nineteenth-century tile boom did go out with a flourish though, with

both impressed and tube-lined tiles in the Art Nouveau style gaining enormous popularity in the early years of the twentieth century.

After World War I decorative tile production decreased significantly, and a decline in church building again led to the demise of the inlaid floor tile. Maw produced interesting ranges of bold abstract Art Deco patterns, but on the whole it was left to a few, often modest companies to continue the tradition of designer tiles. Carter of Poole employed illustrators and artists, such as Edward Bawden, to design period scenes, usually hand-painted or stencilled. Small companies like Dunsmore and Packard and Ord carried on the design tradition beyond World War II.

From the 1920s the hand-craft tradition in English pottery was revived by Bernard Leach (1887–1979), who made some fine plastic tiles. Working in an artistic environment in St Ives, Cornwall, he drew inspiration from traditional Chinese and Japanese ceramics. In Europe a number of important avant-garde painters were decorating tiles, either designing for a manufacturer, as did Salvador Dali, or painting onto a potter's blanks, as did Matisse, or becoming involved in the ceramic process, as sometimes did Picasso. In England John Piper (1903–93) worked with the Fulham Pottery, producing screen-printed designs into the 1980s.

As in America, the widespread revival of hand-craft in the past two decades has extended to tile-making, which has seen an energetic revival. Some have continued to decorate commercial blanks, such as Kenneth and Ann Clark, who developed an impressive range of glaze colours. Others, like Alan Caiger-Smith, who was influenced by De Morgan, or Diana Hall, with her encaustic processes, have built on the Leach tradition.

The range of techniques used today by tile designers is as varied as ever, and the dazzling spectacle of tile making that follows can only serve further to inspire. Whether we already have an interest in tiles or are setting out to have a go at making or studying them, the pages of this book reveal a wealth of traditional qualities and new ideas.

CHAPTER TWO

GETTING STARTED

Lynda Curtis
Condah. 1992
14x10in
(35.6x25.4cm)
PHOTOGRAPH BY
VAN BLERCK PHOTOGRAPHY

Frank Giorgini
Sea Turtles. 1991
6x6in (15.2x15.2cm)

Elizabeth Grajales
Untitled. 1993
7½x8½in (19.1x21.6cm)

PHOTOGRAPH BY BOBBY HANSSON

KILNS

The *kiln* is the heating chamber in which clay is *fired* (or heated) to irreversible hardness and is the most important piece of equipment in the tile-making process. A kitchen oven can't do a kiln's job; its temperatures aren't high enough to cause the chemical reaction that turns clay into a hard material. Once you understand the kiln's function and purpose, you will find it much easier to make and decorate your tiles.

Usually, clay tiles are fired twice in the kiln, first in what's known as a *biscuit firing* and then in a *glaze firing*. The biscuit firing both hardens the tile and makes it easier to handle (dry, unfired clay is brittle and fragile). The glaze firing melts the glaze that's on your tile into a protective, glass-like coating. (For more information on firing your tiles, see chapters 8 and 10.)

Kilns differ in several respects. A kiln's size, its firing range, and the fuel that it uses – electricity, gas or a solid fuel such as wood – may affect the type of tile that you make and the ways in which you decorate it.

An electric kiln, for example, will limit you to what's known as *oxidation firing* – the simple application of heat. A gas-fuelled kiln, on the other hand, offers *reduction firing,* in which the ratio of air to gas is adjusted at certain stages to give a fuel-rich and oxidation-starved atmosphere. This atmosphere brings out specific colours in clays and often results in spectacular and unique stoneware glaze colours that *break* (or disperse) over the surface of the clay. (The bluish orange glaze on my *Turtles* tile – shown above – is an excellent example.) With creativity and practice, however, you should be able to achieve equally satisfying results with an electric kiln.

Firing ranges (the temperatures to which a given kiln is capable of firing) also vary from kiln to kiln. A small, electric test kiln that runs on household current may have a lower firing range than a large commercial kiln; the test kiln may not provide the high temperatures required to fire some clays and glazes. This limitation, however, won't be of much concern to the novice tile maker.

The temperature within a kiln is monitored by means of *pyrometric cones*. These are small, pyramid- or bar-shaped pieces of clay that are manufactured to melt at specific, designated temperatures. When you fire the kiln, you'll usually make up what's known as a *cone pack* (Photo 1) and position it inside the kiln. This is a wad of moist clay into which are placed one or more cones. When the kiln is fired, the cones melt, one at a time, as the kiln temperatures rise. By watching the cone pack through a peephole in the kiln, you'll be able to gauge the kiln temperatures visually.

1

Almost all electric kilns can be purchased with a *cone sitter.* This is a small mechanism that functions in conjunction with a pyrometric cone to turn the kiln off when the interior temperatures reach a specific point. A bar-shaped or small rectangular cone is inserted into the sitter, where it rests on two prongs. A lever rests on top of the cone. As long as the cone remains solid, it prevents the lever from moving downwards, but when the cone slumps,

Suzanne DeMott Gaadt
Celtic Knots. 1992
4x4in (10.2x10.2cm)

George Handy
Untitled. 1993
8x8in (20.3x20.3cm)

one end of the lever lowers, the other end rises, and a hook at that end releases a latch which flaps down, smacks a button, and shuts off the kiln.

Cone packs should always be used as a safety precaution, even when the kiln has an automatic sitter. *Pyrometers* (electric temperature gauges) are also available; these read the kiln temperatures electronically. Cones, however, are more accurate. Electric kilns should also be equipped with a timer with a safety override.

In order to use the kiln's interior space efficiently, you'll arrange your tiles on *kiln furniture* – shelves and holders made from a ceramic material that won't melt during the firing. Kiln furniture accessories are available to accommodate tiles. In the upper left-hand corner of Photo 2 is a block-shaped tile-setter unit with small shelves for individual tiles; to its right is a stacking unit; and shown in the foreground are two types of corner holders.

2

If you don't have a kiln of your own, the best way to gain access to firing facilities is by taking a pottery or ceramics course at your local college or university. You'll also find expert help there when you need it.

Part-time and evening classes at adult education centres are another possibility. Holiday courses in pottery are also available at centres around the country. Places that run courses may also be able to advise you on where you can fire your handmade tiles. Your clay supplier may also have firing facilities.

If you don't have access to any firing facilities, consider purchasing a small, electric test kiln. Many of these operate on household current and are reasonably inexpensive. Though their interiors may provide less than 1cu.ft (.028cu. m) of space, in combination with the appropriate tile setters, they are capable of firing ten or so 4x4in (10.2x10.2cm) tiles at a time. And when you're first getting started, you'll gain more experience by firing a small kiln often than a big kiln less frequently. Firing a test kiln will let you experiment – and learn – faster. Even after you've become a pro, you'll use your test kiln often to obtain quick results on small samples of clay or glazes.

If you do purchase a kiln, be sure to refer to the manufacturer's instructions before you fire it for the first time; kilns vary greatly in their methods of operation. You should also be extremely careful to set it up properly. Don't place a kiln in your living space; the chemicals given off during firing can be toxic. Instead, place the kiln in a separate room or outbuilding and make sure that it's properly positioned and well ventilated (see chapter 16). A small electric test kiln should be placed at least 3ft (91.4cm) away from combustible materials and at least 1ft (30.5cm) above the floor. Protect the floor with an asbestos-substitute, fireproof covering.

CLAY

The clay that you'll be using to make the tiles described in this book is a composite of natural, earthen materials that turns hard when it is fired. It's usually sold in 25lb (10kg) or 56lb (25kg) plastic bags, is moist, pliable, and ready to use, and can be purchased from pottery suppliers or some craft outlets. If it's kept in its moist state, this clay will last indefinitely and will actually improve with age. When it dries out, it can be processed back to its plastic state by crumbling the dry pieces and adding water. (For reasons of health, you should be careful when you do this; see chapter 16 for details.)

Many types of clay are available, each with its own properties and firing characteristics. Your choice of which type to use will be influenced by several factors, among them the type and purpose of the object you're making and the hardness that results from the particular clay's firing range. Colour and texture are also considerations. A basic understanding of clay types and clay firing will help you to select wisely.

The chemical definition of clay is hydrated silicate of aluminium. *Primary* (or *residual*) *clays* are pure clays and are closest to this definition. Like all clays, primary clays are formed through the geological weathering of igneous rocks, but unlike other types of clay, they don't travel far from their source. China clay, from which porcelain is made, is a primary clay; it typically fires to whiteness.

Most other clays are classified as *secondary clays*. After decomposing from the parent rock, these clays are transported by water and ice to a new location, picking up impurities such as minerals and organic matter along the way and usually ending up as a sedimentary deposit at the mouth of a river or at the bottom of an ocean.

Though not as chemically pure as primary clays, secondary clays are more plastic. In addition, their impurities cause them to fire to many different colours in an earthern range of greys, tans, browns and reds. Iron oxide is the most common impurity that results in these variations of

colour. The reddish colour of terracotta, a secondary clay, results from its iron oxide content.

In selecting a clay, your primary consideration will be the *clay body* (the nature and proportions of its ingredients). For tile work, your best choice will probably be a *sculpture* or *modelling body*, which has a fair amount of *grog* (prefired and pulverized clay) in it. A clay that's identified as a *throwing clay* won't be as good a choice because it will contain little or no grog. The grog, which makes the clay slightly gritty to the touch, will give your tile strength and will help to keep it from warping. High-fire porcelain, which has a low grog content, will yield beautiful whites and will provide a good base for bright glaze colours, but porcelain is prone to warping when used in the format of a flat tile.

You will also need to consider the clay's *cone-firing range*, the upper range of temperatures to which a given type of clay can be fired. This range is often indicated by the symbol ∆ and is established according to an industry-standardized temperature-rating system. A stoneware ∆ 10 clay, for example, can be fired up to 2300°F (1260°C).

Appendix A on page 137 provides temperature equivalents for each cone-firing range for Orton cones. Notice that the cone-firing numbers run from cone 022, a very low temperature range, up to cone 11, a very high range.

When a clay is fired to the upper end of its firing range, it reaches *maturity,* the stage at which its molecular structure becomes extremely dense and the clay becomes nonporous, waterproof, and glass-like. The firing range, and therefore the maturity point, of a given clay will vary depending upon the clay's composition. *Earthenware clays* such as terracotta, for example, which are low firing (usually below 2000°F or 1093°C) and porous, will mature at much lower temperatures than *stoneware clays* – hard and

Opposite page: Susan Beere
Aquarium. 1991
18x32in (45.7x81.3cm)
PHOTOGRAPH BY HUGH L. WILKERSON

Above left: Heather Blume
Bonfire Tile. 1992
4x4in (10.2x10.2cm)
PHOTOGRAPH BY HEATHER BLUME

Above right: Nawal and Karim Motawi
Celtic Knot. 1992
8x8in (20.3x20.3cm)
PHOTOGRAPH BY NAWAL MOTAWI

Right: Bettina Elsner
Terra Cotta 'Carpet'. 1989
48x36in (121.9x91.4cm)

Above: Barbara Schwartz
*Night Turns into Day –
Life of the Artist*. 1990
18x28in (45.7x71.1cm)

Left: Carrie Anne Parks
Vines. 1991
28x21x4½in
(71.1x53.3x11.4cm)

Joseph A. Triplo
Dining Room Table. 1991
Without leaves: 40x71in
(101.6x180.3cm)
PHOTOGRAPH BY DAVE PALMER

dense clays that fire above 2000°F (1093°C).

A clay's maximum firing temperature is known as its point of *vitrification.* When the clay is fired at temperatures any higher, it will deform and eventually melt down to become a hardened puddle on the kiln shelf. (Note that kiln furniture, described earlier, is made from a material that won't reach its vitrification point before your tiles do. Kiln furniture is rated for high or low firing. If you're going to be firing in the stoneware range, be sure that your kiln furniture is rated for high temperatures.)

Firing temperatures may also affect the clay's colour. Terracotta will fire to many different shades of redness. When it's fired to 1841°F (1005°C), it turns rosy red, but when the clay is fired to its maturity point – around 2075°F (1135°C) – its colour deepens to brown.

The glazes with which you'll cover your tiles also have firing ranges. A 1841°F (1005°C)/1922°F (1050°C) glaze, for example, is a standard low-fire glaze. For information on glazes and underglazes, see chapters 7 and 9.

The way in which you intend to use your tiles should also be considered. Your tile may not need to be fired to maturity in order to be functional. If you were making a tile for a living-room wall, firing the clay to a non-porous, waterproof state would not be necessary. You might select a stoneware clay, which could be successfully fired to sufficient hardness at lower temperature ranges than those required for vitrification. A clay with a low-fire temperature range – a standard biscuit-firing range of 1841°F (1005°C)/1922°F (1050°C) – would be adequate. If you were making floor tiles, you would probably choose a low stoneware clay, with a 2075°F (1135°C) range up to high-fire stoneware 2300°F (1260°C), for strength.

For exterior installations in wet areas, your tiles must be brought to the vitrification point or very close to it. Even with a glaze over its surface, a tile fired at a lower range can absorb moisture through its unglazed back surface, and this moisture will discolour the glaze or cause it to flake off. If you selected a stoneware 2300°F (1260°C) clay and biscuit-fired your tile up to 2075°F (1135°C), painted a low fire glaze 1841°F (1005°C) onto it, and then fired it to 1841°F (1005°C), the resulting tile would be strong enough for indoor use on a floor or wall, but the clay body itself would still be somewhat porous because the clay was never fired to its point of vitrification – 2300°F (1260°C). You wouldn't want to use this tile in a continually wet area such as a shower wall.

A lower-firing terracotta, on the other hand, could work very well in an outdoor environment. Though the vitrification point of this clay might be as low as 1135°F (2075°C), if you fire the clay to that point, it will become non-porous.

You'll usually be able to get help selecting a clay at a pottery supplier, and the recommendations offered by the people there will be especially important if you don't have a kiln and plan to use their firing facilities.

TOOLS AND EQUIPMENT

As well as a kiln or access to one, you will need some basic pottery tools (shown on the lower left-hand corner of the canvas in Photo 3 on page 26). Though these items can be bought separately, your local pottery supplier or craft shop is likely to carry a packaged set, including a *potter's needle,* a *potter's knife,* a wooden *cutting tool,* a wood *rib,* a *modelling wire* and a sponge. To make your first flat clay tiles, you should also have the items in the list that follows.

Two strips of wood, 3/8in or 1/2in (1cm or 1.3cm) thick
Pieces of canvas

Libby Donohoe
Siena Deer. 1992
4x15¼in (10.2x38.7cm)

Sections of smooth board or wall-board, about 16x20in (40.6x50.8cm)
Rolling-pin
Metric ruler
Straight-edge
90° angle or square
Pencil
Cardboard or Masonite
Sheets of clear plastic or plastic bags

As you begin to experiment with different tile-making and glazing techniques, you'll also want to have other tools and supplies on hand. Each of these is described in subsequent chapters, and with the help of the information in chapter 14, you'll be able to make many of these items yourself. Others are technique-specific, so wait until you decide which techniques to try before you spend your hard-earned money.

WORK SPACE

For beginners, who will be working on a small scale, a complete studio won't be necessary, but if you don't have access to a classroom or commercial studio, you'll need to set up a space of your own – one that isn't a part of your living space. Clay dust and glaze materials must be kept out of your home. An outbuilding is ideal; a garage or a basement with good ventilation and a separate entrance can be used at a pinch.

Your studio should have a flat working surface and running water, and it must be well ventilated. Once you start making large quantities of tiles from moist clay, it will also need to be large enough to accommodate shelves or *drying racks* (similar to baking racks) to hold boards stacked with drying tiles, as well as accumulated glaze supplies and additional tools.

Making use of a college or professional pottery studio can be an economical and space-saving alternative to gradually taking over your own property. If your budget is tight and you don't have a vacant outbuilding, enroll in a pottery course!

Important safety guidelines are provided in chapter 16; read them carefully. And as you set up your studio and work in it, keep three basic rules in mind: Work 'wet', clean 'wet', and clean compulsively! Your goal is to avoid creating clay dust. When you can't avoid it, remove it without stirring it up. Wipe down your tools and all horizontal surfaces frequently with a damp sponge, and plan ways to prevent yourself bringing any dust into your home. Make sure that your space is well ventilated. Wear surgical or plastic gloves and an appropriate BSI-approved mask that will filter mist and dust when you're using glaze chemicals. Whether the glazes are in powdered or liquid form, many of the colourants in them are composed of toxic metallic oxides.

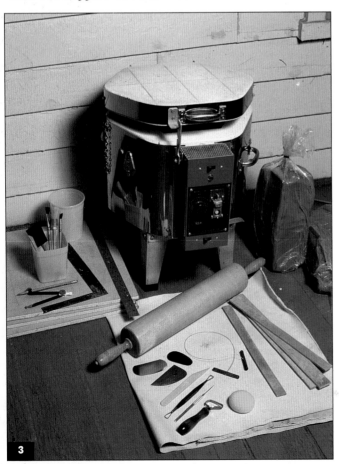

3

MAKING A FLAT TILE

Tamara Jaeger
Moroccan Stars. 1991
6x6in (15.2x15.2cm)
PHOTOGRAPH BY CHAS KRIDER

Natalie Surving
Sea Turtle. 1991
4x4in (10.2x10.2cm)

Frank Giorgini
Afro Tile. 1992
12x12in (30.5x30.5cm)
PHOTOGRAPH BY BOBBY HANSSON

MAKING A SLAB

To make tile shapes, you'll first need to cut a chunk of moist clay from your large bag and roll it out into a slab. Start by spreading out a piece of canvas or stretching it over a flat board. Peel back the plastic from the bag, and using your cutting wire, slice off a 2in- to 3in-thick (5.1cm to 7.6cm) chunk of clay (Photo 4). Place the chunk on the canvas-covered board. Make a habit of removing the moist clay that's left on the wire by running two fingers along the wire (Photo 5) and pushing the clay that you collect back into the bag or into your work. If you don't, these bits of clay may dry out, fall off the wire and crumble into clay dust – something to be avoided.

Then, using the heel of your hand, pound the slab into a roughly flat shape. If you like, you can help flatten and stretch out the slab by picking it up and tossing it at an angle against the canvas-covered board. Next, select two strips of wood, both ³/₈in or ¹/₂in (1.0cm or 1.3cm) thick, and place one on each side of the slab. The sticks should be parallel to each other and spaced no further apart than the length of your rolling-pin (Photo 6).

Lay another piece of canvas on top of the slab and

strips. Rest the rolling-pin on top of the covered strips (Photo 7) and start rolling. The canvas will keep the rolling-pin from sticking, and the strips will ensure that the entire slab is rolled to a uniform thickness. Remember, if this method is to be effective, that the rolling-pin should be moved back and forth across the strips until it rides evenly along their full length (Photo 8).

Kathy Triplett
City Hall (from Pack Place series). 1992
Each 8x8in
(20.3x20.3cm)
PHOTOGRAPH BY KATHY TRIPLETT

When you're making a large number of tiles, a *slab roller* (Photo 9) comes in handy, but beginners certainly don't need to purchase this piece of equipment. The slab roller produces slabs of uniform thickness by forcing clay between two horizontal cylinders or under one cylinder. It's a large piece of of equipment and will require a large portion of your work space, but it will also serve as a very

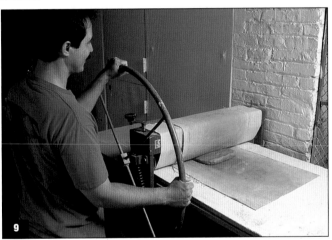

effective work table when it's not being used for slab production. Slab rollers come with manufacturer's directions for use; read them carefully.

TRANSFERRING THE SLAB

In order to measure, cut and dry your tiles, you'll need to transfer the slab to another flat surface. If you cut your tiles to shape on the canvas and then have to transfer them from it, you will run the risk of deforming them. Moving the slab now will also free up your work table for rolling out more slabs.

There are several ways to transfer the slab. If you've rolled it out on a canvas-covered wooden board or piece of wall-board, place a piece of wall-board on top of the slab. (A wooden board can be used for this purpose, but the moisture that it absorbs from the slab will cause it to warp. Covering this wooden board with canvas or with several layers of newspaper will help to prevent moisture absorption.) Then flip over the sandwiched slab. The slab will now rest upside down on the wall-board.

If you've rolled a texture into the surface of the slab (see page 58) and want that original, textured side to face up,

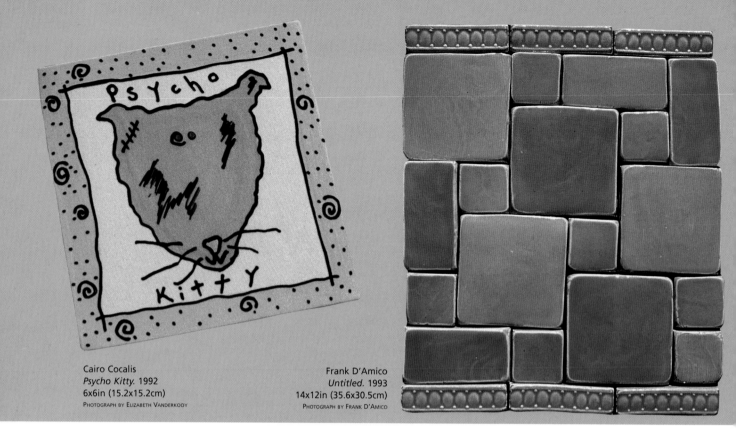

Cairo Cocalis
Psycho Kitty. 1992
6x6in (15.2x15.2cm)
PHOTOGRAPH BY ELIZABETH VANDERKOOY

Frank D'Amico
Untitled. 1993
14x12in (35.6x30.5cm)
PHOTOGRAPH BY FRANK D'AMICO

just repeat the procedure with another piece of wall-board. (Note that pieces of wall-board or wooden boards should be discarded as soon as they begin to retain clay or the clay no longer separates cleanly from them. The clay dust that old boards are likely to trap can be hazardous to your health.)

If your slab rests on canvas only and isn't supported by a board, proceed as follows. After placing a piece of wall-board on top of the slab, lift one end of the canvas, holding it tightly against that end of the board. As you flip the slab over, it will flex with the canvas; bend and stretch it as little as possible. Though clay should relax flat, it sometimes has a 'memory', and even if you flatten the deformed slab again, it will be more prone to warping during the later drying and firing stages.

Attempting to lift the slab with your fingers may cause it to stretch, deform, or even rip. If you don't have wall-board or wooden boards on hand, place flat sticks above

10

and below the slab (two rulers will work) and hold the slab gently between them as you lift (Photo 10). By spreading out the pressure needed to hold the slab, you'll minimize distortion of the clay.

CALCULATING SHRINKAGE

Because clay shrinks as it dries and again as it is fired, your original tile must be larger than the size that you want your finished tile to be. Every clay has a different *percentage of shrinkage*; each will shrink a different amount depending upon the temperature to which you fire it. For these reasons, you'll need to calculate the shrinkage of the particular clay that you're using.

Catalogue descriptions of purchased clay will usually indicate the percentage of shrinkage at a designated firing temperature. In general, the higher the temperature to which the clay is fired, the greater the shrinkage. Clays with more grog or *filler* (sawdust, straw or sand, for example) usually shrink less than others.

The most accurate way to determine shrinkage at a particular temperature is to make clay *test strips* and fire them. Roll out a small slab of the clay from which your tiles will be made and cut it into several strips, each about 1½in (3.8cm) wide, 6in (15.2cm) long, and ⅜in to ½in (1.0cm to 1.3cm) thick. (See the next section, 'Cutting Tile Shapes', for instructions on the cutting process.) With a metric ruler, measure and mark each strip at 10cm, as shown in Photo 11. Metric measurements will make calculating percentages much easier.

Before you test fire each of these strips at a different temperature, use your pin to mark the soft clay with the cone number to which you'll be firing that strip. You may also want to note the type of clay body from which the strip was made (cone 10 stoneware or cone 6 modelling

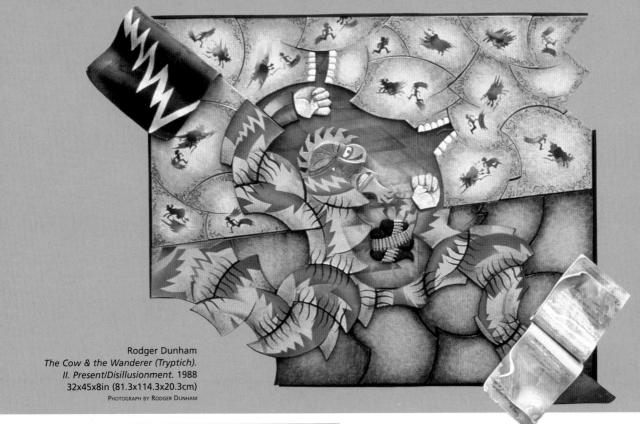

Rodger Dunham
The Cow & the Wanderer (Tryptich).
II. Present/Disillusionment. 1988
32x45x8in (81.3x114.3x20.3cm)
PHOTOGRAPH BY RODGER DUNHAM

body, for example). Marking the strips will enable you to keep track of the results of your test firing.

After each of the test tiles has been fired (for firing instructions, see chapter 8), measure its length again. Then calculate the percentage of shrinkage. If the 10cm mark is now 8.8cm long, you have 12% shrinkage (100mm – 88mm = 12mm; 12mm = 12%).

The next step is to calculate how large to cut your tile in order to end up with a finished tile of the size that you want. The example that follows includes the formula that you'll use.

Finished tile size: 4x4in (10.2x10.2cm)
Shrinkage: 12% at desired temperature range

M = Original moist clay tile size
S = Percentage of shrinkage
F = Finished tile size

Use the formula $(1 - S)M = F$

$$(1 - 12\%)M = 4$$
$$(0.88)M = 4$$
$$M = 4 \div 0.88$$
$$M = 4.54in\ (11.5cm)$$

As you can see in this example, a 4½x4½in (11.4x11.4cm) original moist clay tile will result in a tile very close to 4x4in (10.2x10.2cm).

With this formula, as long as you know two of the variables, the third can always be calculated. To determine the percentage of shrinkage for an original moist clay tile that is 4½x4½in (11.4x11.4cm), for instance, and a finished tile size of 4x4in (10.2cm), just use the formula as follows:

$$(1 - S)M = F$$
$$(1 - S)4.5 = 4$$
$$1 - S = 4 \div 4.5$$
$$1 - S = 0.88$$
$$1 = 0.88 + S$$
$$1 - 0.88 = S$$
$$0.12 = S$$

The percentage of shrinkage is 12%.

CUTTING TILE SHAPES

To cut standard square or rectangular tiles from your rolled slab, you'll need a straight-edge, a ruler, a large 90° angle or square, and a potter's needle. Unlike a knife, the needle (with which you'll scribe the slab and cut the tiles) won't veer off course if your hand twists while you're using it. A knife tends to cut toward the angle at which the blade's surface is twisted; a needle, on the other hand, has no directional preference.

Before cutting your square or rectangular tiles, first visualize how to get as many as possible from the oval

Kathy Triplett
Crab (right) and *Deco Crab* (left). 1993
Each 6x6in (15.2x15.2cm)
PHOTOGRAPH BY KATHY TRIPLETT

slab. Next, to make a grid on the slab, use your pin and straight-edge to measure and scribe parallel lines every 4$\frac{1}{2}$in (11.4cm) or the desired length of a moist tile. Do this until you run out of space. Now use the angle or square to scribe perpendicular lines every 4$\frac{1}{2}$in (11.4cm) or the desired width of a moist tile. Check your measurements, and then, using the straight-edge and potter's needle, cut all the way through the scribed lines (Photo 12). Peel away the excess slab, wedge it up while it's still soft, and place it in a plastic bag for re-use.

12

To make patterns for geometric tile shapes, draw the shape on a large sheet of graph paper. Then place the paper pattern on top of the clay and transfer its lines by making a series of pin pricks through the pattern lines on the paper or by running a rounded pencil point along them. (Photo 16 on page 38 shows the pin-prick technique.) Remove the graph paper when you've finished and use your needle to cut all the way through the slab at the marked lines. The same method can be used to transfer non-geometric designs; just use ordinary paper instead.

Another accurate method for cutting flat tile shapes is to cut a *template* (or pattern) from a piece of cardboard or thin Masonite. Then, for each tile that you plan to cut, use your needle to trace the template's outline onto the rolled slab. It's also possible to fabricate pastry-cutter type tools for cutting shapes; see chapter 14 if you'd like to make your own. These tools are often equipped

with a plunger that releases the tile from the tool.

When you want to repeat an intricate pattern of individual tiles – ones that aren't necessarily square – making a plaster mould of one section of the pattern can be helpful. By pressing the mould onto the slab, you will imprint outlines of the tile shapes that lie within that area of the pattern. (Instructions for making plaster moulds are given in chapters 4, 5 and 6.)

For a unique and free-form effect, you can try cutting your tiles directly from the block of moist clay, as shown in Photo 13. By wiggling the cutting wire as you slice off each slab, you will create a texture in the clay surface. If you'd like to try this technique, first pound the bag of clay into a shape that's roughly 4$\frac{1}{2}$x4$\frac{1}{2}$in (11.4x11.4cm) or the desired shape of your moist tile. Even with this loose technique, don't forget to calculate shrinkage. When cutting several textured tiles in this manner, alternate flat cuts with textured cuts in order not to waste any clay.

After the tiles have been cut, try not to handle or bend them too much; they're usually still soft. Smooth off their rough top surfaces by running your finger along each one.

13

Right: Ellie Stein
Miriam and her Tambourine. 1992
48x36in (121.9x91.4cm)

Below: Beth Starbuck and Steven Goldner
Skybars and Trapezoids (detail). 1992
48x36x1in (121.9x91.4x2.5cm)

If the clay is still too soft, wait awhile before doing this; you don't want the pressure from your finger to squash the tile.

Your tiles may look flat at this stage, but will they stay that way? Herein lies one of tile making's greatest challenges. In fact, the biggest problem most beginners have is getting their tiles to dry and fire flat. Though your tiles may never attain the flatness and perfection of commercial *dust-pressed* tiles, which are made by compressing dry clay particles with hydraulic machinery, that's not what handmade tiles are about. It's reasonable, however, to aim for a tile that isn't warped.

DRYING THE TILES

Green ware, whether it is decorated with underglazes or not, must be dried before it can be fired. As you read this section, keep in mind that different decorative techniques for green ware are executed at different stages of dryness. Before you tackle these techniques, described in the next few chapters, you'll find it helpful to understand the tile-drying process.

When the clay is partly dry and as stiff as a thick piece of leather but contains some moisture and is still workable, it is called *leatherhard*. A leatherhard tile isn't flexible, but if you press your fingernail into its surface, the clay will retain an impression.

When the clay is *bone dry,* it will appear uniformly light in tone and will be dry to the touch. It will also be at room temperature and will rapidly absorb a drop of water placed on its surface. Bone-dry tiles are delicate and brittle, so handle them with care. And to avoid producing clay dust, don't scrape or sand them. Scraping and sanding are best executed on leatherhard tiles.

If tiles are left to dry rapidly on a wooden board, their upper, exposed surfaces usually dry faster (and shrink faster) than their bottom surfaces, and the tiles warp. Sculpted tiles' thinner edges may also dry at a different rate than their inner portions, causing warping as they do. Most shrinking and warping of tiles is a result of rapid moisture loss during the early drying stages; drying tiles slowly will help to prevent these problems.

One way to ensure slow drying at a controlled rate is to cover your tiles with a sheet of plastic for a day or so and then loosen the plastic so that air reaches the tiles slowly. While you're waiting for one project to dry and firm up, just tackle another. Or, if you're executing a decorative technique that is best completed on leatherhard tiles and you have a large batch of tiles to complete, you can keep them from becoming bone dry as you work on them one at a time. This will eliminate 'down time' by allowing you to work on more than one project at a time.

The best method for producing really flat tiles, however, is to place rows of freshly cut tiles between layers of ½in-thick (1.3cm) wall-board and then stack the boards in three or four layers (Photo 14). If you've cut your tile shapes from slabs placed on pieces of wall-board, all you'll need to do is stack these boards. The paper-covered plaster sheets absorb moisture evenly from both the tops and bottoms of the tiles, and the pressure created by the stacks helps to flatten the tiles. Avoid making the stacks too tall; the weight of too many tiles and boards may restrict shrinkage and cause undue stress. Of course, this method will only work for flat-surfaced tiles.

Don't cover these stacks with plastic unless you plan to be away for a few days and wish to prolong the drying process. When the tiles are in the latter stages of leatherhardness, they can be removed from the boards and set on a wooden shelf, another board, or any flat surface and left to continue drying in the open air, or they can be wrapped in plastic to maintain their leatherhard state. To help prevent warping, you may also stack the leatherhard tiles face to face, one tile upside down on top of another tile of the same shape.

You'll soon realize that success in working with clay is all in the timing. If you try to handle your tiles when they're still too soft, you will bend and squash and deform them. If you wait too long, the tiles may get too dry and brittle, and that certain technique that you wanted to try will no longer work.

CHAPTER FOUR

MAKING TILE MODELS
FOR OPEN-FACE PRESS MOULDS

Frank Giorgini
Floral. 1993
12x12in (30.5x30.5cm)
PHOTOGRAPH BY BOBBY HANSSON

Heather Blume
Wave Motif. 1986
12x12in (30.5x30.5cm)
PHOTOGRAPH BY HEATHER BLUME

Diane Winters
From the *Arabesque* series. 1991
Each 4x4in (10.2x10.2cm)

RELIEF TILES

Relief tiles, unlike the flat tiles described in chapter 3, are tiles with three-dimensional designs on their surfaces. Because designing and sculpting an original handmade relief tile takes a great deal of time and work, it makes sense to create an *open-face press mould* (a plaster mould of the original tile) with which you can press out multiple replicas of the tile.

Your single-tile design can be a complete composition in itself – one that is meant to stand alone – or can represent one unit or section of an overall graphic pattern that is formed when that unit is arranged with others exactly like it.

The original tile is a positive *model,* one that's used to make an open-face plaster mould and that is sometimes destroyed during the process. The mould will be a negative shell of the original positive tile model, and the tiles that are produced with the mould will be positive replicas of the original tile.

Tile models for the open-face press-mould process can be made in many ways; *layering* and *direct carving* are two.

THE LAYERING TECHNIQUE

The layering technique, one way to create a high-relief tile model for an open-face press mould, lends itself to hard-edged bold relief and graphic designs. Tiles made with this method usually look very sculptural and architectural.

First, you'll need to work out a design. Let's assume that you'd like to come up with a composition consisting of identical tile units that will be arranged next to one another. Following is a technique that may help you to visualize your overall design.

Draw a series of 2x2in (5.1x5.1cm) squares on a piece of standard graph paper. Imagine that each of these squares is a single tile; you have as many chances to dream up a single-tile unit as you have squares on your page.

Next, draw a different design in each square. Remember that each square represents an entirely different design concept; you'll choose only one, which will then become the single-tile design upon which your composite design is eventually based. Keep the different designs simple and let one idea flow into another.

When you've filled the page, make ten to twelve photocopies of it. Then cut each 2in (5.1cm) square; you'll now have ten to twelve squares for each design that you created. In order to visualize your overall design, play with each set of identical squares, manipulating the individual squares to form a complete design. Take a look at Photo 15, in which you'll see a composite design in the lower left-hand corner; a single tile unit is in my hand. You'll be surprised by how quickly patterns evolve with the various arrangements of these design units.

As you work with this technique, keep in mind that while your tiles don't have to be square, a square tile can be oriented in four different directions, a triangle in three, and a rectangle in only two. It's fun and informative to play with with the tile cut-outs in this way.

Once you have selected a design, transfer it, enlarging it to its full size, onto another sheet of paper. It's easiest to do this on a photocopier, but it's also possible to do by hand. If your small tile cut-out is 2in (5.1cm) square, for

Diane Winters
Geometric Rope. 1990
Each 3¾x3¾in (9.5x9.5cm)

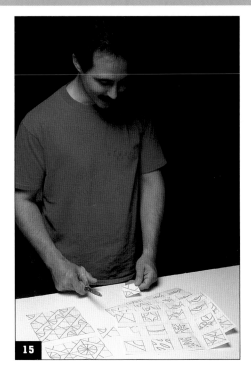

15

example, and you'd like your tile to be 8in (20.3cm) square, draw a new square – one in which there are four graph units for every one unit in the old square – on a new sheet of graph paper. Then redraw the pattern into the new square by copying the contents of each small graph unit on the old sheet into each four-unit section on the new sheet. If you want your fired tile to be a specific size, don't forget to calculate and take into account the percentage of shrinkage.

Decide how many layers your relief design will require; two or three levels are sufficient for most relief designs. You may find it helpful to colour, shade, or otherwise mark each section of the finished pattern to designate that section's level. You'll notice that if two design areas of the same level are next to each other, they become a new shape – a combination of the two. You may therefore have to alter the designated levels so that each shape is defined by its vertical (relief) edges.

Next, roll out as many slabs of clay as there are layers in your design. For a three-layered design, roll two slabs that are each about ³⁄₁₆in (.5cm) thick and one slab about ³⁄₈in (1.0cm) thick. For a two-layered design, beginners might want to start with a ¹⁄₂in-thick (1.3cm) bottom layer and ¹⁄₄in-thick (.6cm) top layer. These slabs should be about 2in (5.1cm) longer and 2in (5.1cm) wider than the full size of the individual moist tile. If your tile design is 8¹⁄₂x8¹⁄₂in (21.6x21.6cm), for example, each slab should be roughly 10¹⁄₂x10¹⁄₂in (26.7x26.7cm).

To make a three-layered design, you'll stack the three slabs on top of one another and then carve away sections of each slab to create your relief design. Consider this fact before you decide whether to smooth off each slab's surface, leave the canvas texture on it, or roll another texture into it (see page 59). If the middle layer, for example, has a texture on it, once you've removed the uppermost layer, the texture will be visible.

After the slabs have set up for about thirty minutes and their surfaces are no longer sticky, layer them on top of each other, placing the thickest one on the bottom and setting the stack on a board that can be placed on a turntable.

Hanna Lore Hombordy
Shells and Sand. 1991
14x16in (35.6x40.6cm)

Next, centre the sheet of graph paper with your full-sized tile design on top of the layered pile, making sure that all four edges of each slab extend beyond the perimeter of the design. You wouldn't want to discover, after you'd trimmed the excess clay away, that your design stretched beyond the outer edge of one of the hidden slabs.

To transfer the design, use a potter's needle to pierce through the graph paper along each design line (Photo 16). When a design line extends right to the edge of the tile's perimeter, visualize the line continuing beyond that perimeter and poke an additional hole into the slab outside the perimeter. As you connect the inner dots by scribing over them, you may obliterate some; these outer dots will provide you with reference points if you do. Both the transferred design lines and reference-point dots are shown in Photo 17.

It's also possible to transfer your design by tracing over the paper pattern with a pencil; the pressure will leave a depression in the clay. This method, however, won't leave as clean an edge once you've cut along the line on the clay. A slight indentation may still be visible after you've sliced through the line's centre. Now remove the graph paper, use a potter's needle to connect the dots (Photo 18), and you're

Ellie Hudovernik
Sheep on Canopy Bed. 1993
6x6in (15.2x15.2cm)
PHOTOGRAPH BY ROBERT HUDOVERNIK

Susan Beere
Egret's View. 1991
36x24in (91.4x61.0cm)
PHOTOGRAPH BY HUGH L. WILKERSON

mould. Thinking of your model as a series of pyramids may help. The edges of every level of the design should angle upwards and inwards. If you place a light directly over the model, no shadow should appear on any edge of the design.

ready to cut. To make the cuts, use a knife with a fine blade. A No. 11 craft-knife blade will work well on all but the thickest tiles. For these, use any sharp, fine-bladed knife. As you cut the design into the tile model, the most important thing to remember is to avoid undercuts. The sides of each cut design section should be angled slightly outward – 5° to 10° from perpendicular – so that each raised relief area is wider at its base than at its top surface. In Photo 19, note the angle at which I'm holding my knife. If the edges of the design's raised portions are angled incorrectly (inwards), the undercut areas will fill with plaster when the mould is poured and will make it impossible to release the clay model from the hard plaster

Opposite page, left:
Renée Habert and Jim Stonebraker
Rabbit/Dog. 1993
9x9in (22.9x22.9cm)
PHOTOGRAPH BY BOBBY HANSSON

Opposite page, right: Arnon Zadok
City Tile. 1987
4x4in (10.2x10.2cm)
PHOTOGRAPH BY BOBBY HANSSON

Left: Beth Starbuck and Steven Goldner
Pinwheel Pentagons (detail). 1986
50x36in (127x91.4cm)

Below: Frank Giorgini
Dark Dawn. 1985
Mounted mural: 28x42in
(71.1x106.7cm)
PHOTOGRAPH BY JOHN LAWRENCE

Hold the knife just as you would hold a pen. Rather than shifting your hand to make cuts on different portions of the tile, just spin the turntable so that – for right-handed people – the design area is always on your right. Grip the knife rigidly, keeping it at the proper 5° to 10° angle and draw it towards you as you cut. Locking your hand, wrist and arm into a rigid position and moving your whole body backwards will help you to control the knife; it's surprisingly easy to cut a straight line at a constant angle when you use this method. Practice helps, of course!

Cut the perimeter of the tile first and then the inscribed lines of the interior design. Keep checking the angle of your knife so as not to undercut. If you're right-handed and are cutting lines on the left side of the stacked slabs, the top of the knife blade should be angled slightly towards the right. In more complicated designs, the directions of the angles can get tricky, but once you understand the principle of layering, you'll have no trouble working them out. To facilitate cutting curved lines, keep your knife stationary and rotate the turntable instead.

Don't worry about accidentally cutting too deeply into the lower layer while you slice through the one above it. Unless you slice all the way through the lower layer, these accidental cuts are not a problem. They'll leave thin fins of plaster on your mould, but these fins are easy to remove. The real problem comes from not cutting deeply enough, which will create a ragged, torn edge when you remove the layers.

Now comes the exciting part. Starting with the top layer, poke into the exposed edge of a design section that needs to be removed and then carefully peel it away. Once you've removed the unwanted sections from the top layer, use the same cutting-and-peeling method to remove the unwanted sections from the middle layer (Photo 20),

working down towards the base layer, which should remain uncut unless you plan to create a hole in your tile.

Remember, each edge of each section that remains should angle downwards and outwards from its own top surface.

Though the layering technique just described lends itself to hard-edged geometric designs, it can also serve as a basic starting point for any type of relief design. If you'd like to create a realistic animal figure, for instance, begin with three stacked slabs and then carve and round them off. This method will help you to get a feel for carving in relief. (The *Rabbit/Dog* tile shown above was made in this manner.)

Your clay model is now ready to cast into a plaster mould. Because you haven't wet, scored and adhered the layers of this model together as you would have if you were direct carving a single tile for firing, the layers would separate if they were dried and fired. The model that you've just made, however, won't be dried or fired. Instead it will be discarded after you've made a mould with it. See the next chapter for mould-making instructions.

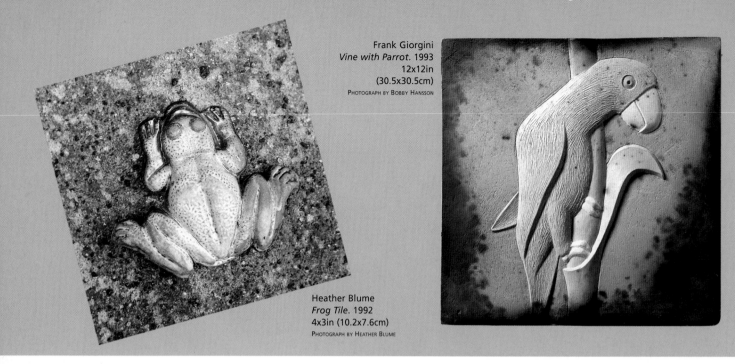

Frank Giorgini
Vine with Parrot. 1993
12x12in
(30.5x30.5cm)

Heather Blume
Frog Tile. 1992
4x3in (10.2x7.6cm)

THE DIRECT CARVING TECHNIQUE

In direct carving, the moist clay model is actually sculpted. Similar models can be made with wax or oil-based clay, neither of which will shrink as you work with them. If you enjoy working with moist earthen clay and are accustomed to it, however, you might prefer to stick with it. Do remember not to mix oil-based clay and water-based clay; the results would be disastrous.

Once you've selected a design, transfer it onto a rolled-out slab of clay. The slab should be wider and longer than your design, because you'll be whittling away at it. In fact, you will need to add even more clay to the amount that is necessary after shrinkage has been taken into account. If your finished tile will be 4x4in (10.2x10.2cm), for example, and shrinkage calls for a 4^1/$_2$x4^1/$_2$in (11.4x11.4cm) moist tile, roll out a 5^1/$_2$x5^1/$_2$in (14.x14cm) slab.

Because you'll be adding clay to this tile, as well as removing it, roll your slab to about three-quarters the thickness of your finished tile; the cut slab should be about as thick as the middle ground of your design.

Now scrape clay away from the background areas and build up the elevated areas by adding more moist clay. Mastery of the layering technique described in the previous section will help you to visualize the transformation of a two-dimensional paper design into a three-dimensional bas-relief tile. A tile at three stages of direct carving is shown in Photo 21.

For scraping, pushing and shaping the clay into the desired shapes and contours, use various bamboo or wooden *modelling tools*, *scraping tools* such as knife blades and sections of hacksaw blades, and *hooped turning tools*. (In chapter 14, you'll find directions for making some of these tools yourself.) Dental instruments are useful for creating fine details; ask your dentist if he or she has any available.

When you're building up areas of the tile, always score the slab's surface with a potter's needle, add a little water

21

or clay slip (which acts as a glue) to the scored surface, and then press the additional moist clay on top. (See page 62 for a description of clay slip.) Be sure to press the added clay down well; you don't want to trap any air between the upper and lower pieces. You can make a slip that shrinks at the same rate as your tile model by collecting the little scraps that you trim off tiles made with the same clay. Let these scraps dry to bone dry, put them in a plastic bucket, and mix them with some water. The result will be a slip of the same composition as your clay body.

When the clay is too soft, only rough shaping (the first stage of sculpting) is possible. To make the clay more workable, cover the model with plastic and let it set up overnight. As it loses moisture and approaches leatherhard it will be easier to refine its surface design.

When you have completed your tile model, keep it under plastic until you are ready to mould it. To keep it in its leatherhard state, just spray it intermittently with water. If you let the clay get bone dry, you'll find it difficult to return it to its leatherhead state, so keep an eye on it. As long as beads of moisture are forming under the plastic, the tile is sufficiently moist.

The next step is to make an open-face press mould from your layered or carved model.

CHAPTER FIVE

MAKING AND USING OPEN-FACE PRESS MOULDS

George Mason.
Variation. 1991
34x34in (86.4x86.4cm)
PHOTOGRAPH BY DENNIS GRIGGS

43

George Johnson
Table and Bench. 1993
Table: 72x36in
(182.9x91.4cm)
Bench: 36x36in
(91.4x91.4cm)
PHOTOGRAPH BY BOBBY HANSSON

PREPARING THE MODEL AND FORM

Now that you've created a tile model, the next step in the open-face press-mould process is to make a plaster mould. You do this by assembling a form around your model, mixing plaster, and pouring it into the form.

First, transfer your leatherhard model from the surface where it was shaped to a smooth, non-porous surface. Place the edge of a wooden ruler on one side of the tile and gently push the tile off onto a thick piece of glass or formica. Secure the model by gently pressing it in place. If the model is too dry and seems to slide on the smooth surface, just dampen its back a little with a sponge and press it down again. If the model doesn't adhere properly to the surface, the force of pouring the plaster over it may cause it to shift its position.

In order to contain the liquid plaster mixture that you'll pour over your model, you'll need to build a *plaster mould form* to place around it (Photo 22). These forms are referred to as *cottles* (or walls) and are made from wood or plastic. They are held together with C-clamps, straps or threaded rods. (For instructions on how to make a plaster mould form, see chapter 14.) The cottles must be high enough and sturdy enough to contain the plaster, and you must be able to adjust them to fit the tile. To calculate the height of the form, add 1¹/₂in to 2in (3.8cm to 5.1cm) to the depth of the highest surface of the clay model. Pieces of standard 2x4 are often suitable; their 3¹/₂in (8.9cm) width provides a convenient form height.

Adjust your mould form to leave about 1¹/₂ to 2in (3.8cm to 5.1cm) between each side of the tile model and the inside surfaces of the form. Secure the form and seal all its corners by pressing a thin coil of clay along its inside bottom edges and into its inside corners (Photo 23). If you're using deep-walled cottles, make a reference mark in the soft clay in one corner, about 1in (2.5cm) above the

highest part of your model. This mark will tell you how much more plaster to add once the model itself has been submerged.

Next, you may need to coat the working surface and the inside surfaces of the form with a *release* (a substance that will prevent the plaster from sticking). Mould soap, petro-

Cynthia Lyons
Trout Tile. 1993
6x6in (15.2x15.2cm)

Dale Wiley
Mola. 1988
6⅝x6⅝in (16.8x16.8cm)

leum jelly, vegetable oils and spray lubricants will all work. Plaster won't stick to clay, so you won't have to apply release to the model itself. Clean glass, formica and varnished wood release very well with a minimum of lubricant, but a surface like unfinished wood requires a generous coating of release.

When you've secured your tile model on the glass, adjusted your form around it, and sealed and coated the inside of the form with a release, you'll be ready to create a negative mould of your work by mixing and pouring plaster into the form.

MIXING AND POURING THE PLASTER

Plaster (a powdered, semi-hydrated form of gypsum which, when mixed with water, recrystallizes to a hardened state) is the preferred material for mould making. Interestingly, the term *plaster of Paris* is derived from the first recorded use of plaster by potters, in early eighteenth-century France.

Contemporary tile makers often use *potter's plaster*. This material can be obtained from your clay supplier; it comes in 50lb (22.7kg) and 100lb (45.4kg) bags. Be sure to store plaster in a dry place; its shelf life is limited by its tendency to absorb moisture.

Hydracal is another, stronger moulding material, one often used by experienced tile makers. This substance can be used alone or mixed with plaster in a one-to-one ratio. A mould made with Hydracal will be stronger than one made with plaster but will also be less absorbent, so your tile will not release from the mould as quickly.

To calculate the necessary amount of plaster, first refer to Chart I, which provides rough sizes for mould forms and the necessary amounts of water and plaster to mix for each form. Use the water weights as your reference. The plaster weights are accurate, and it's a good idea to have

at least as much dry plaster on hand as the chart indicates is necessary, but the plaster-mixing method that you are about to learn doesn't require you to pre-measure the plaster that you use. You'll be gauging the amount of plaster by eye, instead, in a technique known as the *'island' method*.

Note in this chart that the amounts of plaster and water are based on the amount of mixed plaster required to fill an empty mould form. Your tile model will displace some of the mixed plaster, so you'll have some plaster left over.

CHART I

Plaster Mixing

Size of Mould-Form Interior	Pounds (Kg) of Water	Pounds (Kg) of Plaster
8x8x3in (20.3x20.3x7.6cm)	4.5 (2.0kg)	7 (3.2kg)
9x9x3in (22.9x22.9x7.6cm)	6 (2.7kg)	9 (4.1kg)
10x10x3in (25.4x25.4x7.6cm)	7 (3.2kg)	11 (5.0kg)
11x11x3in (27.9x27.9x7.6cm)	9 (4.1kg)	13.5 (6.1kg)
12x12x3in (30.5x30.5x7.6cm)	10.5 (4.8kg)	16 (7.3kg)
13x13x3in (33.0x33.0x7.6cm)	13 (5.9kg)	19.5 (8.6kg)
14x14x3in (35.6x35.6x7.6cm)	14 (6.4kg)	21 (9.5kg)
15x15x3in (38.1x38.1x7.6cm)	17 (7.7kg)	26 (11.8kg)
16x16x3in (40.6x40.6x7.6cm)	20 (9.1kg)	30 (13.6kg)

The ratio of plaster to water determines the strength and absorbency of your finished mould. A standard mixture is about 100 parts of water to 140 parts plaster. Specific technical formulas and charts are available for mixing plaster, but for our purposes, the age-old island method will work just fine. Here's how to use it.

Place the required amount of cold tap water in a clean plastic bucket. The bucket should not only be large enough to hold the required amount of water and plaster, but should also leave you ample space for stirring and mixing the two together. Adding plaster to the water will increase the volume of the bucket's contents by about 50%. If the bucket is filled to 6in (15.2cm) with water, for example, adding the plaster will raise the level of the contents to about 9in (22.9cm).

Before you begin to mix in the plaster, you should have on hand a watertight receptacle or another prepared form; you'll need to pour any leftover plaster into one of these containers so that it doesn't harden in the bucket. You should also mix up a ½ cup (118.4ml) test batch (see the mixing instructions that follow). Wait to see how this small batch of plaster sets up; if it never gets hard, throw your dry plaster away and begin again with a fresh bag. Plaster can become stale if it lies around the studio for a long time.

You'll only have about one to four minutes' pouring time, depending upon the condition of your plaster mixture, so be sure to prepare your model and mould forms before you begin. Wearing a dust mask and rubber gloves, sprinkle the plaster steadily across the entire surface of the water in the bucket, allowing the plaster to sink as you do. If the plaster has lumps in it, sieve it as you pour it into the water.

Continue to add plaster until islands of plaster begin to form above the water's surface. Stop sprinkling until the islands are absorbed and then add a little more. Wait again for the islands to be absorbed and add more. These waiting periods are called *slaking;* tap the bucket during slaking in order to make any air bubbles rise to the surface. At first, the islands will sink into the water very quickly. As you continue, however, they'll take longer and longer to be absorbed. Stop adding plaster as soon as the islands sit for ten to fifteen seconds before they're absorbed.

Then mix the solution carefully, using your fingers to squeeze out any lumps. To avoid creating air bubbles, keep your gloved hands submerged. Continue blending until the mixture is the consistency of single cream. You'll have a minute or so to complete the mixing; don't panic, but do work at a steady pace. As soon as the plaster turns from a single cream consistency to a double cream consistency, it's time to pour it.

Pour the plaster into the mould form slowly and steadily, aiming for the area between the tile model and form and letting the plaster flow steadily over the model (Photo 24). Fill the form to the desired thickness, about 1in to 1½in (2.5cm to 3.8cm) above the model's upper-

24

most surface. Jiggling the table gently will help the plaster to settle into the model's nooks and crannies and will also release any trapped air bubbles. Pour the excess plaster into the extra form or waterproof container.

Don't worry if the plaster that you've mixed is a little thin. Your mould will just take a little longer than usual to dry. Plaster that's too thick is more problematic; it will begin to harden before you get a chance to pour it and will flow out in lumps as you do. Plaster this thick won't pick up fine details from your tile model.

CLEANING UP AND FINISHING THE MOULD

Wipe the excess plaster on the sides of the bucket down towards the bottom. Immediately add about a cup (236.8ml) of water and rinse the inside of the bucket by swishing its contents around. Then pour the contents into the waterproof container, where they'll settle to a semi-hard state and can be disposed of along with solid waste. (Pouring the rinse down the sink would clog the drain.) Now sponge and rinse your mixing bucket thoroughly. If you wait to clean it, any remaining plaster will harden, and the bucket will be very difficult to clean.

You'll notice that plaster gives off heat as it hardens; this is a result of the recrystallization process. After it has reached its highest temperature and has hardened (in thirty to forty-five minutes), remove the mould forms and then scrape and clean them.

Slide the hardened plaster mould off the glass surface and flip it over so that the bottom of your clay tile model is visible. Gently peel out the soft clay (Photo 25), using a wooden tool, if necessary, to lift the edge of the model from the mould. Be careful not to nick the inside of the mould. You'll probably have to discard the clay model, but you'll now have an exact, negative plaster replica of your

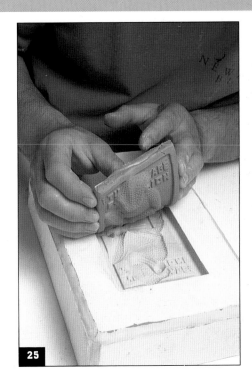

25

tile. By filling its negative space with moist clay, you can make literally hundreds of replicas of your original tile.

To dry the mould, first place a couple of sticks – uniform in size – on a drying shelf or board. Then place the mould on the sticks, with its negative (hollowed) side facing down. The mould may take a week to dry sufficiently. To accelerate the drying process, place the mould in a warm dry place or in front of a fan.

When the mould is completely dry, round off all its outside corners with a rasp; rounded edges are less likely to chip. They also look neater and make people think you know what you're doing. Make sure that the back of the mould is smooth and flat.

On the mould's inside surfaces, you may notice thin fins of plaster sticking up out of your design. These are created when plaster flows into deep cuts left in the clay by your knife. Just break the fins off with your fingers. Use a wooden tool for any other trimming, but don't rush to do too much. It's better to press out your first tile replica and then determine if other adjustments to the mould really need to be made.

MAKING CLAY PLUGS FOR THE OPEN-FACE PRESS MOULD

The next step is to press moist clay into the negative mould and pop out a positive replica of your original tile model. Start by dusting out the dry plaster mould with a clean, soft brush. Place it face up on a smooth, ¾in-thick (1.9cm) bed of unwrinkled newspapers or flat cardboard; folded ridges in the newspaper or cardboard bed may cause the mould to crack when you pound on it.

Then make a *plug* (or slab) of soft clay that is a little thicker than the deepest part of your mould and just large

enough to fit into the opening in it. Just use the slab-cutting and rolling method described in chapter 3.

If you plan to make many plugs of the same size, you may want to use a *slab cutter* to cut them. (Photo 26). This

tool, which can easily be made from scrap materials (see chapter 14 for instructions), will cut your preparation time in half when you're cutting multiple slabs of identical thicknesses. It operates by cutting uniformly thick slabs from a newly opened bag of clay, making it unnecessary to roll out clay slabs with a rolling-pin or slab roller, a process that often takes longer than it does to press the tile itself.

To use the slab cutter, begin by slamming four sides of a sealed bag of moist clay down onto your work table until the top end of the clay block is roughly the size of the desired plug. Then place the bag on end and carefully peel back the plastic. Position the slab cutter face down on the clay and draw the taut wire towards you by pulling it along the protruding metal or wooden edges. The wire will slice off a clay slab of uniform thickness. Remove the slab and place it on a piece of canvas. Repeat this process until the entire block has been sliced into plugs.

Next, using a potter's needle and a template that is just the size of the opening in the mould, cut each plug to shape. Then wedge up the trimmings and cut a few more plugs from them. Stack the plugs, placing pieces of canvas between the layers. Cover the stack with plastic so that the tiles are kept moist until you're ready to use them. By first forming clay plugs in the correct sizes and thicknesses, you can press out tiles faster and more efficiently.

Opposite page, left:
Nawal and Karim Motawi
Leaves and Berries. 1993
8x8in (20.3x20.3cm)
PHOTOGRAPH BY NAWAL MOTAWI

Opposite page, right:
George Mason
Untitled. 1993
12x16in (30.5x40.6cm)
PHOTOGRAPH BY DENNIS GRIGGS

James and Patricia Evanko
Ceramic Tile Installation. 1993
16x30in (40.6x76.2cm)
PHOTOGRAPH BY PATRICIA J. McGARRY

PRESSING THE PLUGS INTO THE MOULD

Place a plug in the mould (Photo 27) and tap it down gently with the palm of your hand, working from the centre to the corners and making sure that the plug fills the mould's edges and corners. Then place a piece of cut canvas over the clay and pound the clay down by striking the

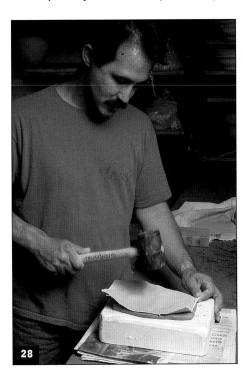

After you've packed the clay into the mould, fold up the squashed-out clay edges. Stretch your cutting wire taut between your hands and draw it back towards you, along the mould's top surface (Photo 30). This will remove the

canvas with a rubber mallet (Photo 28). Again, try to make sure that you're forcing the clay into the edges and corners. (Use clean canvas if you can. If your canvas has dry clay residue on it, mist the surface with water to keep the dust from rising as you pound with the mallet.)

Next, place a small block of wood on top of the canvas and really wallop it down with the mallet (Photo 29). Move it to another area above the mould opening and hit it again. Repeat this process until the entire area has been pounded into the mould. Be careful not to hit your fingers.

Nawal and Karim Motawi
Old English Rabbit. 1993
6x6in (15.2x15.2cm)
PHOTOGRAPH BY NAWAL MOTAWI

Frank Giorgini
Rhino. 1993
6x6in (15.2x15.2cm)
PHOTOGRAPH BY BOBBY HANSSON

excess clay fairly close to the mould's back surface. To smooth off the surface even more, take a rigid, straight stick and scrape it across the surface of the tile (Photo 31). Work from the middle of the tile towards the edges, or you'll distort the clay by pulling it away from the edges of

31

the mould opening. When the stick passes smoothly across the entire surface, the back of your tile is flat.

Now is the time to incise or stamp your name or logo into the back of the tile. Then place a smooth block of plaster (the back of another mould or a couple of pieces of wall-board will do) over the top of the mould and set it aside to dry. The weight of the plaster block on top and the plaster surrounding the clay will help the tile to dry and shrink evenly. (For instructions on how to make plaster blocks, see chapter 14.)

Depending on the condition of the mould and on the complexity of your design, the tile should be ready for removal between fifteen minutes and an hour later. Simple, open, shallow designs will release more quickly than complex, deep ones. Check the mould periodically. When the clay's edges start to separate from the mould, your tile can be released. In most cases the tile shouldn't be allowed to dry completely in the mould because it will shrink and crack around the mould's solid, raised sections.

To remove the tile, place two narrow strips of wood or

corner moulding, approximately ¼in (6cm) thick, on the edges of the mould, making sure that the strips don't cover the clay tile. Then place a sturdy board (face down) on the wooden strips, flip the whole assembly over, and tap the top of the mould.

The tile may slip right out (Photo 32), but it's more likely that you'll have to exert a little force to help it along. Tap the mould's edges, above the wood strips, with a rubber mallet. Don't hit the middle of the mould or you might crack it. If this doesn't release the tile, try lifting one edge of the board up about 2in (5.1cm) and slamming it down onto a sturdy table. This procedure could raise

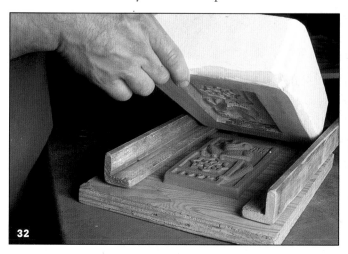

32

some dust, so keep all your tools and equipment clean.

Keep peeking into the space between the board and the mould to see whether the tile has fallen out of the mould on all sides. Once it has, remove the mould and the sticks and press the tile gently down to make sure that it's lying flat. Tapping the board down on the table will also settle the tile down flat. You now have an exact replica of your original tile model.

Next, transfer the tile to a piece of wall-board to dry. Push it onto the board by gently pressing against a length of wood placed against the side of the tile. The tile can be left to dry at this point. If it warps, refer to pages 34 and 54 for techniques that will help you to avoid this problem in the future.

CARVED PLASTER BLOCKS, TILE PRESSES AND PUGMILLS

Carol Susan Clemens
Two Day. 1992
17x22in (43.2x55.9cm)

MAKING A CARVED PLASTER BLOCK

This method of pressing out a tile differs from that described in the previous chapter in that the negative design is sculpted directly into a plaster block; no tile model is necessary (Photo 33). In addition, tiles made with the carved-block technique, unlike those made with an open-face press mould, do not need to dry and shrink before they're released from the block. For these two reasons, the carved-block method is considerably faster, especially if you use a tile press instead of pressing the tiles by hand.

33

Note also that a carved block is as long and as wide as the actual tile that you press with it. Unlike the flat border area of an open-face press mould, which serves only as a restraint, the flat area of a carved plaster block is an active part of your tile design; the flat background of your tile will be pressed by it. The raised relief sections of your finished tile will be shaped by the block's carved sections.

First, you'll need to make a block of hardened plaster, about 1½in (3.8cm) thick and shaped to the desired size

of your tile before (not after) shrinkage. For instructions on how to make several of these blocks at one time, see chapter 14.

Tools for scraping and gouging, such as those used in linoleum-block cutting and engraving, are useful, as are looped turning tools, a potter's needle and a knife.

There are several ways to transfer your design to the surface of the plaster block. The method that you choose will depend in part on whether your design is symmetrical or asymmetrical. If the design is symmetrical, just draw or trace it directly onto the block. An asymmetrical design – one that incorporates letters or numbers, for example – will have to be transferred in reverse as a mirror image of the original design. One way to do this is first to use a soft pencil to draw the design on paper. Then flip the paper over, place it face down over the block, and rub over the back of the paper to transfer the graphite pencil markings to the surface of the white block.

A similar transferring technique is shown in Photos 34, 35 and 36. First, copy the design to the correct size on a commercial photocopying machine. Place the copy on the block with its printed side facing down. Then dab the back

34

Opposite page:
Diane Winters
Iris and *Dianthus*.
1992
Each 4x4in
(10.2x10.2cm)

Right: Lloyd Reiss
Reflection. 1993
5½x5½in
and 6x6in
(14x14cm
and 15.2x15.2cm)
<small>PHOTOGRAPH BY BOBBY HANSSON</small>

35

36

Next carve the design. Remember that the areas you carve away will appear as raised sections on the surface of your pressed tile. If you find this concept visually confusing, check your progress as you carve by periodically pressing a wad of soft clay into the surface of the plaster block (Photo 37). In general, carve down a maximum of about half the thickness of the background tile base. If

37

you're carving relatively deeply, keep the grooves wide enough to allow the clay to be pressed all the way down into them.

It's possible to make a similar press block from biscuit clay instead of from plaster by incising or impressing a low-relief design into a leatherhard tile and then biscuit firing it. This biscuit tile can be used to press soft clay tiles; their designs will be mirror images of the original tile design. The photos at the top of this page show the results of this technique. Plaster-block moulds are stronger than these pressing tiles, and the clay will release more easily from them, but if you want to avoid working with plaster and have limited production in mind, a pressing tile can be an adequate alternative.

of the copy with a ball of cotton wool that has been wetted with nail-polish remover. (Use non-acetone removers only; they're much less hazardous to your health.) The photocopier ink will transfer right onto the block. Unfortunately, this method doesn't work as well on leatherhard clay as it does on plaster.

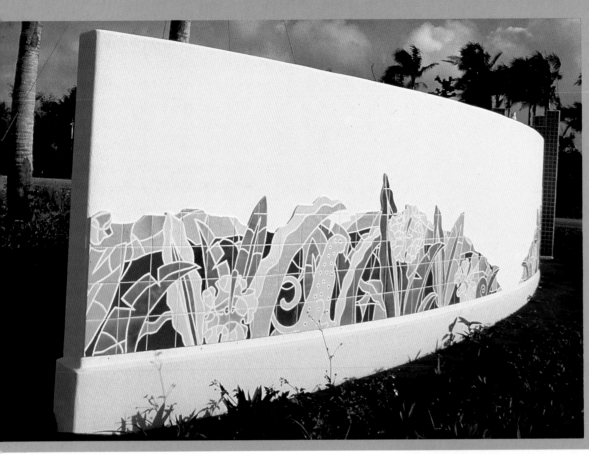

Opposite page: Diane Winters
Untitled. 1990
Each 5x5in (12.7x12.7cm)

Left: Diana and Tom Watson
Design by Sussman Prejza
*Leo Palace Resort:
Daro Road Sign*. 1993
36x312in (91.4x792.5cm)
PHOTOGRAPH BY BIELENBERG

PRESSING TILES BY HAND

There are two ways to use your carved plaster block to create the relief surface on your tile: pressing by hand and mallet or pressing with a tile press, a tool that is described in the next section.

To press your tiles by hand, first place the carved block face up on a cushioning bed of newspapers. Then cut a slab of clay that's the same length and width as the block; you can trace around the block itself. The thickness of the slab should be slightly greater than the thickness of your finished tile, including its relief portions. For a very shallow relief – $^1/8$in (.3cm), for example – the slab shouldn't be much thicker than the finished tile. For a $^3/8$in-deep (1.0cm) carved design, the slab might be $^1/2$in (1.3cm) thick. If you find that your slab is too thin, just roll out one that's a little thicker.

Next, place the slab over the block and position a piece of canvas on top of the slab. Then, on top of the canvas, place a wooden board that's about the same width and length as the plaster block. If the board is too large, you'll have a difficult time keeping it level as you pound it. If your carved block is exceptionally large, perhaps 18in (45.7cm) or longer, use a small wooden block first, moving it around the surface as you pound, but finish up with a large block.

Tap the wooden block down with a mallet so that the resulting tile is of uniform thickness. When the tile is the desired thickness, trim away the excess clay by running your pin around the block's perimeter. Then carefully peel the tile from the block, trying not to bend it as you do. You should have an exact positive impression of your carved design (Photo 38).

38

Place your pressed tiles on a board or piece of wallboard, cover them with plastic and let them dry for a day or so. To complete the drying, gradually pull back the plastic, letting more and more air get to the tiles. (Drying boxes can be purchased, but it's easier to build a wooden frame and surround it with plastic instead.)

A variation on the carved-block technique is shown in Photo 39. The plaster blocks on the left-hand side of this photo were actually cast right from the surface of a relief pattern. Like a carved block, a mould cast in this manner is the same width and length as the moist clay tile that is pressed with it. In the example shown, a plastic replica of an architectural moulding was cut to about 6in (15.2cm) in length. Cottles were set up flush with the edges of the plastic model, the mould was sealed with moist clay from the outside (not the inside), and the plaster was mixed and poured as explained in chapter 5. Tile designs sculpted from moist clay can also be cast in this manner, and the moulds that result also work well in a tile press.

Both the carved-block technique and the variation

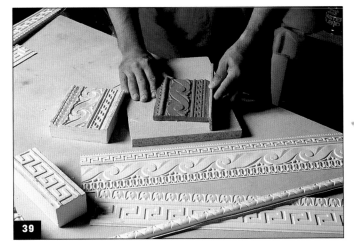

39

just described are most appropriate for smaller tiles – approximately 20 sq. in (129 sq. cm) or less – the relief designs of which are low. For deeper, larger tiles and those with raised borders around the edges of their designs (see Photo 32 on page 50), make an open-face mould instead. If you attempted to create a tile border by using a carved block, you would have to carve a negative depression along the rim of your plaster block. Then, when you tried to use the block to press moist clay, the clay would tend to ooze out around the edges of the block; there would be no restraining border of plaster to force the clay back into the carved design areas. For this reason, the open-face mould technique is better suited for tiles with borders.

USING A TILE PRESS

Combining the carved-block technique with the use of a hand-operated *tile press* provides a very quick and efficient method of producing detailed relief tiles. Studio tile presses are available commercially – there are even hydraulic studio models – but the hand-operated tile press shown in Photo 40 is the one that I designed and built myself. Instructions for making one just like it can be found in chapter 14. The simple lever-and-vertical-plunger design allows the user

40

Fired Earth Tiles
Fossil: Aquamarine. Ongoing
Each 4^5/$_{16}$x4^5/$_{16}$x3^3/$_8$in
(11x11x9cm)

to apply an incremental amount of pressure to the block – evenly, quickly and efficiently. The press can also be used with open-face press moulds, but the tile size should be limited to 20 sq. in (129 sq. cm) or less.

To use the tile press, place a board on the base of the press and cover it with a piece of canvas. Place the slab of clay on the canvas and the carved block (face down) on the clay. On top of the block, position a layer of cardboard to serve as a cushion. Be sure to centre the block and clay under the plunger. Then pull down once on the tile-press plunger, pressing the block down into the clay until the tile is the desired thickness. Turn the board and everything on it around 180° and pull the plunger down again. Doing this will help to compensate for the inevitable variations in pressure.

When you're making multiple tiles with the tile press, establishing a rhythm to your movements can speed up the process considerably. Pull the board out from under the plunger, remove the cardboard, and use your potter's needle to trim the excess clay from the perimeter of the block. Pick up the block and peel the pressed tile off it. Then set the block aside and place the tile on a board, pressing the tile down gently to make sure that it's flat. Bend the tile as little as possible during this process. Return to the press and start again. The quick process of pressing, trimming and releasing each tile from the block will enable you to really crank out the tiles.

At a certain point, the carved block will begin to get moist, and peeling the tiles from it will begin to be more difficult. When this happens, dry the block in front of a fan and take a break, or use another block while you let the damp one dry for fifteen to twenty minutes. If you let your clay slabs dry out for a few minutes before pressing the carved block into them, this will also help to keep the clay from sticking. Don't let them get too stiff, or pressing will be too difficult.

When the pressed tiles are leatherhard, trim their rough edges with a trimming tool. Then, using a damp sponge, stroke outwards to smooth away any scrape marks.

PUGMILLS

A *pugmill* (Photo 41) is a tool that squeezes moist clay through a die in order to produce a relief design. The tool includes a lever-and-plunger mechanism, a *barrel* (or chamber) into which the moist clay is placed, and inter-

changeable dies, each with a specific pattern cut through it. Dies for basic studio-model pugmills are cut into plywood, plastic or metal.

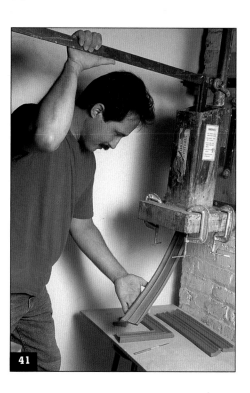

41

To operate the pugmill, follow the manufacturer's directions. The basic process is simple. Fill the barrel with clay, select and attach a die to the bottom of the barrel, place the plunger and lever on top of the tool, and pull down on the lever. The pressure in the barrel forces moist clay through the shaped opening in the die. The linear form that is extruded can be cut at spaced intervals to yield individual tiles.

This tool is especially useful for making mouldings, *bullnose edges* (to wrap around outside corners), inside corners, and flat tiles with a linear-relief surface design. With the right die in place, the pugmill can even produce hollow shapes such as tubes or pipes. *Quarry tiles*, the floor tiles often seen in business environments, are usually produced by large hydraulic pugmills in the tile industry. The upper surfaces of these tiles are flat and their bottom surfaces are ribbed; the ribbing helps the tiles to dry flat and to adhere better once they're installed.

Chapter Seven

Surface Decoration on Unfired Tiles

Hanna Lore Hombordy
Evening Breezes. 1991
26x35in (66x88.9cm)
Photograph by Hanna Lore Hombordy

Linda R. Ellett
Geometric Pattern (detail). 1989
Each 5x5in (12.7x12.7cm)
PHOTOGRAPH BY LINDA R. ELLETT

Linda R. Ellett
Geometric Pattern (detail). 1989
Each 5x5in (12.7x12.7cm)
PHOTOGRAPH BY LINDA R. ELLETT

STAGES OF TILE DRYNESS

In this chapter, you'll find information on decorative techniques that are performed before your flat or relief tiles are biscuit fired. Some of these methods work best on clay in its moist state, others on clay at the leatherhard stage, and still others on bone-dry clay. Appendix B on page 137 offers some guidelines as to when each of these techniques should be executed.

TRANSFERRING THE DESIGN

There are a number of ways to transfer your design to an unfired tile, some of which have already been discussed. One method is to use a pencil to draw the design direct onto the leatherhard or bone-dry tile. Pencil lines on green ware will usually burn off in the firing. If the tile is still a little soft and has not yet reached the advanced leather-hard or bone-dry stage, however, your pencil point will probably leave an indentation in the tile's surface. This may, or may not, be desirable.

Special *underglaze pencils* that won't burn off, as well as pastel *underglaze crayons* (usually for use on biscuit ware), are available. The crayons are actually underglazes in a non-liquid form; they may be used on green ware, on top of a painted underglaze, or on unglazed biscuit.

You can also use tracing paper to trace the design onto a tile in its leatherhard stage. Place the paper (face up) on the tile and trace over it with a dull pointed tool; a pin tool or blunt pencil will work. The tool will impress a line into the soft clay or, as is shown in Photo 42, into a coat of underglaze that has already been applied to the tile.

A fourth method for transferring designs involves piercing holes in the design lines on your paper in order to leave dots in the leatherhard clay. One disadvantage to this technique is that it will leave visible dots in the clay surface.

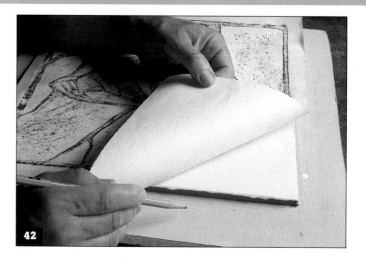

42

Yet another method – a traditional one known as *pouncing* – involves making pin pricks along the design lines on a piece of paper. When the pierced paper has been positioned on the tile, a cloth bag filled with finely ground charcoal is 'pounced' over the pierced holes. The design lines are thus transferred in the form of dots of charcoal dust. In spite of its messiness, this technique is reliable.

IMPRESSING

One of the wonderful properties of clay is its malleability; when it's moist, any object that is pressed into it will leave an impression. At different stages of stiffening, from soft and moist to leatherhard, the tile will exhibit different levels of impression sharpness. Impressing is an effective method of adding interesting three-dimensionality to your tile's surface.

Many objects make good impressions: letters and numbers from old type sets, children's plastic alphabet sets, carved wooden or plaster shapes, and rubber stamps. (Logos can be made into stamps relatively inexpensively.)

Jane W. Larson
Energy and Life (detail of
Chlorophyll panel). 1992
36x360x2in
(91.4x914.4x5.1cm)
PHOTOGRAPH BY RUTH CAREY

Natural objects – leaves, shells, seeds and pieces of wood with interesting grains, for example – can also be pressed into the clay. Even the texture of a piece of cloth or plastic string-bag (Photo 43) can be impressed by placing a cloth or bag over your tile slab and then rolling over it.

Using this technique in combination with the coloured slip inlay method, described on pages 64–66, will result in a beautiful and unique surface. Just impress your design and fill the recessed impression lines with slip.

43

UNDERGLAZES

Underglazes, which may be applied to green ware or to biscuit, are ceramic pigments in liquid form. They derive their name from the fact that they are often covered with glazes, which brighten their otherwise dull and matt colours, affix them to the tile, and provide a glass-like coating over them. Put simply, underglazes go under glazes.

The modified *metallic oxides* in underglazes give them their colour. Cobalt oxides yield blue, for example, copper oxides yield green, and manganese oxides yield black. Underglazes can be mixed by hand, but because the metallic oxides in them are toxic, beginners should work only with pre-

mixed commercial underglazes, available in 4oz (113.4g) jars. When you purchase underglazes, which are relatively inexpensive, check the descriptions on the jars' labels to make sure that you get types that can be applied to either green ware or biscuit.

As well as oxides, underglazes also contain a little *fluxing material.* During firing, the fluxing agent makes the underglaze melt just enough to hold it onto the clay but not enough to become sticky. Note that underglazes, because they don't melt into a glass-like state as glazes do, aren't waterproof, and unless they've been covered with a glaze, they can be rubbed off the tile, even after they've been fired.

PAINTING WITH UNDERGLAZES

Painting tiles with commercial underglazes is one of the most accessible forms of tile decoration. Though designs may be created with either underglazes or glazes, one advantage to using underglazes is that their colours, unlike those of glazes, usually look very much the same on the fired tile as they do in the bottle. (Note that underglaze colours will always be brighter after a clear glaze has been fired on top of them.) Arranging underglaze colours in chromatic relationships to one another as you work is therefore relatively easy. In addition, underglaze colours do not run into one another on the tile as glaze colours do.

As with many other painting mediums, most underglazes of the same type can be blended together before application. Mixing some white with a medium-blue underglaze, for example, will result in a lighter blue. A plastic ice-cube tray makes an excellent underglaze mixing and painting pallet. Underglazes are water soluble; when they dry out in the tray, you can bring them back to working consistency by adding water.

When underglazes are applied to green ware, the clay should be in the latter stages of leatherhard or bone dry. Working with green ware has one disadvantage. Unfired clay is brittle and fragile, while biscuit, which is harder, is somewhat easier to handle. In spite of this fact, many tile makers prefer to apply underglazes to green ware. They feel that by doing so they can obtain a more opaque covering with fewer visible brush marks.

Another advantage to applying underglazes to unfired clay is that it often saves a firing step. Underglaze decoration on green ware is solidified and affixed to the tile by biscuit firing. A clear glaze is then brushed onto the biscuit-fired underglaze, and the tile is glaze fired. If you apply your underglaze to biscuit, an intermediate firing may be necessary because the underglaze hasn't been affixed by heat; brushing glaze over an unfired underglaze may smear it. This is especially true when your work is very detailed. It would be best either to fire the underglaze before brushing on the glaze or to apply the glaze by spraying or dipping.

Applying underglazes to unfired clay has one additional benefit. If you miss any spots as you paint or the underglaze leaves streaks, you'll be able to see them before they're sealed underneath a clear glaze. After the underglaze is biscuit fired onto the tile, wetting the tile with water to make its surface shiny will make any imperfections show up right away. You can then touch up the tile with extra underglaze. If you apply the underglaze to a biscuit tile and then cover it with a glaze, you won't notice the bare spots and streaks and will be stuck with them after the glaze firing.

Note in Photo 44 that the bone-dry terracotta tile was first painted with a coat of white slip. This slip provides a bright background for underglaze colours. (For a full description of slips and their application, see the sections that follow.)

Once your design has been transferred to the surface of the clay (or to the coat of slip), use a brush of an appropriate width to paint your underglaze onto the tile. Always stir the underglaze before you use it and cap the bottle or cover the tray with plastic when it's not in use so that the

underglaze won't dry out. For an opaque covering on green ware, three coats of underglaze are generally recommended. Allow each coat to dry before applying the next.

It's possible to effectively cover and obliterate one colour by painting over it with another. It is also possible to create a light, transparent covering on your tile, similar to those in a watercolour painting, by thinning appropriate underglazes, but thinned underglazes should be applied only to biscuit, not to green ware. An unfired tile's surface will become muddy from the amount of water necessary to achieve this effect.

Opposite page: Rodger Dunham
Untitled. 1991
45 sq. ft (4.18m²)
PHOTOGRAPH BY RODGER DUNHAM

Left: Rodger Dunham
Untitled. 1991
60 sq. ft (5.57m²)
PHOTOGRAPH BY RODGER DUNHAM

Top of page: Ginger Legato
Woman in Water. 1986
72x72in (182.9x182.9cm)

Above: Joan Gardiner
Dolphin (from *Wave Border Design*). 1991
4x7½in (10.2x19.1cm)
PHOTOGRAPH BY SUSAN HUNTINGTON

Natalie Surving
*Tree Frog with
Maple Leaf.* 1991
Each 4x4x⁵⁄₁₆in
(10.2x10.2x8cm)

Affra Gibbs
Rosie. 1992
4¼x4¼in
(10.8x10.8cm)
PHOTOGRAPH BY BOBBY HANSSON

Instead of painting your design with underglazes on green ware, it's also possible to paint the design with glaze colours on biscuit (see chapter 9). Remember, however, that glaze colours will run into each other. If you're aiming for a bright, shiny glaze surface and a multi-coloured, sharp-edged design (one in which different colours don't blur where they touch each other), paint your design with underglazes, biscuit fire the tile, and then follow with a low-fire, clear glaze coating. The tile maker who created the 'baby' tile shown above has made excellent use of painted underglazes to provide a cheerful, playful look.

SPRAYING WITH UNDERGLAZES

For the most subtle shading and colour application, underglaze colours can also be thinned and applied to green ware or to biscuit with an airbrush. With practice and skill, the colours can be worked as effectively as on any airbrush painting. Note that these thinned underglazes won't cause the surface of the unglazed tile to become muddy; a sprayed underglaze mist won't pool on the tile as a thinned and brushed underglaze would. After airbrushing, biscuit fire the tile and then brush on a clear glaze or apply that glaze with an airbrush.

A simpler way to achieve an airbrush effect is to spatter underglaze colours onto the unfired tile with a bristle brush or toothbrush. Try using a flat object (a leaf, for example) as a stencil. Place the object onto the tile and then run your gloved finger across the bristles of a brush that's been dipped into underglaze. Be sure to run your finger towards you so that the spray projects away from you and onto the tile. By doing this, it's possible to build up a pattern of silhouetted shapes on your tile and to create a soft, dotted colour surface. The sprayed design will dry almost instantly. This technique, probably familiar to you from childhood art projects, can yield quite sophisticated results when adult control and creativity are added.

If you've applied your underglaze to bone-dry ware, your tile can be biscuit fired right away. If your tile was leatherhard, wait for it to become bone dry before firing it.

SLIPS AND ENGOBES

You may hear the terms *slips* and *engobes* used interchangeably, but there is a technical difference between the two. Slips, which can be as thin as underglazes or as thick as cake icing, are clay in a liquid form, with or without added oxides or colour pigments. Though slips for biscuit are available, slips are usually applied to green ware at its early leatherhard stage.

Engobes are also liquid clay compositions. Unlike slips, however, they contain *frits* or other fluxing agents that make them melt when they're fired. Frits are pulverized, glass-like materials (also found in glazes), which give a slight sheen to engobes. Engobes do not melt down to a flat and glassy state as glazes do; they retain a raised, drier surface. Glazes, which contain more frit, become much more vitreous during firing.

Note that underglazes are much like engobes but are usually thinner. Engobes can be modified to meet specific needs by varying the amount of each ingredient when they're mixed. Slips usually have more body and thickness than engobes and retain a more raised surface even after firing.

Engobes work best when they're applied to moist and leatherhard green ware. They're not usually applied to biscuit, though by adjusting the amount of fluxing agent in an engobe formula, it is possible to formulate an engobe for fired tiles.

Because both slips and engobes contain a high percentage of clay, they must *fit* the clay bodies to which they are applied so that they dry, shrink and fire at a rate similar to that of the tile. Unless they fit, they may crack or separate from the tile and fall off it. To determine if a proper fit has been achieved, test fire slips and engobes on the clay that you're using. (You may never even get to the test-firing stage; if you apply a slip to a leatherhard or bone-dry tile, and it peels off as the tile dries, you'll know right away that there's a problem with the fit!) Because slips do not contain the fluxing agents that help to attach engobes to clay, their fit becomes especially important. They must go on unfired clay so that they can dry and shrink as the clay does.

Above: Frank Giorgini
Butterfly. 1993
12x12in (30.5x30.5cm)
PHOTOGRAPH BY BOBBY HANSSON

Right: Vivika Heino
Bamboo Tile. 1988
30x18in (76.2x45.7cm)
PHOTOGRAPH BY BILL DOW

Below: Vivika Heino
Fern Leaves. 1993
14½x16in (36.8x40.6cm)
PHOTOGRAPH BY BILL DOW

Slips and engobes are available through many companies. Coloured slips can also be formulated in the studio by adding various oxide stains to a base white slip. Even underglazes can be added to slips to obtain a variety of colours. Beginners should avoid mixing their own formulas, but for experienced potters, slip formulas are provided in Appendix C on page 138.

Both slips and engobes may be applied by painting or spraying. They can sometimes be applied to biscuit tiles by dipping (see chapter 9). Neither slips nor engobes will run, but when you paint them onto your tile, be sure to let each coat dry before you apply the next.

SLIP TRAILING

The method that takes full advantage of a slip's full-bodied properties is *slip trailing* – the application of slip through a tube. This technique is most appropriate for clay in the early stages of leatherhard.

First fill a plastic dispenser bottle, one with a long, narrow neck, with a slip of a colour that contrasts with your moist clay tile. To create a raised surface of dots and lines, squeeze the thick liquid out onto the tile as if you were decorating a cake. Then cover up the tiles with plastic and dry them slowly.

45

46

The unfired stoneware tile shown in Photos 45 and 46 has first been painted with white slip. The design is being slip trailed over that base white coat.

INLAID TILES

In contrast to tiles decorated with underglazes, *inlaid* (or *encaustic*) tiles are decorated by embedding coloured clays or clay slips into the surface of the tile. Because an inlaid design penetrates below the tile's surface, its colours do not wear away. For this reason, inlaid tiles have long been popular as floor coverings. Development of the encaustic method is usually attributed to twelfth-century Cistercian monks, who produced paving tiles for English monasteries.

The coloured clay for inlay work is made by mixing powdered colourants such as stains and oxides with a light-coloured clay base. This is a messy and unpleasant task, so try to purchase pre-coloured moist clays, which are available in 2.2lb (1kg) bags from clay suppliers. The coloured clay, which should fit the clay body of your tile, is then rolled or pressed into recessed design areas on the soft base tile.

One way to create an encaustic effect is first to roll out a clay slab that is the desired thickness of your tile. Then arrange the coils of coloured clay on its surface and use a

Opposite page, left: Bernadette Stillo
Lovers in the Grass. 1992
5³/₄x7³/₄in (14.6x19.7cm)
PHOTOGRAPH BY BOBBY HANSSON

Opposite page, right: Frank Giorgini
Afro Tile. 1993
12x12in (30.5x30.5cm)
PHOTOGRAPH BY BOBBY HANSSON

Right: Otto Heino
Fish Panel. 1984
14½x16in (36.8x40.6cm)

rolling-pin to press the coils into the slab until the surface of the slab is level. You may also use a slab roller to do this pressing job for you.

When using clay slips with the inlay method, it's best to work on leatherhard tiles and to use fairly thick slips. First, incise your design with handmade incising tools or with a notched blade tool, similar to the one used in linoleum-block cutting (Photo 47). (See chapter 14 for instructions on making the former.)

Next, fill in the recessed areas with clay slip. If your design lines are many, you may want to use a wide brush to coat the whole tile with slip first (Photo 48). When that coat of slip has dried slightly (in about fifteen minutes),

48

coat will shrink as it dries. Continue to apply the slip until it builds up in the areas over the incised design and protrudes above the original tile surface.

Let the tile and slip dry to the advanced leatherhard stage. Then use the edge of a metal rib to scrape off the excess slip (Photo 49) until you reach the uppermost surface of the original tile (Photo 50). You'll achieve a cleaner finish if you scrape in the same direction as the inlaid slip or clay rather than scraping perpendicular to those lines.

47

49

repeat the process until the slip has built up over the incised design.

If the incised design lines are shallow and few, just dab the slip into the grooves. Keep adding slip; the previous

Left: Frank Bosco
Day Dream. 1989
47½x47½x1½in
(120.7x120.7x3.8cm)
PHOTOGRAPH BY BARRY PRIBULA

Above: Frank Bosco
It Only Happens Every Time. 1990
48x47x1½in
(121.9x119.4x3.8cm)
PHOTOGRAPH BY BARRY PRIBULA

Scraping the tile when the clay is still soft will smear its surface, but scraping a bone-dry tile will produce more clay dust than is good for your health. Scrape only when

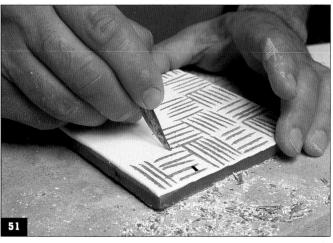

the tile is leatherhard. Be sure to wear a dust mask when you do this and to collect the scrapings for disposal.

Narrow incised lines don't usually provide problems. If your inlay design incorporates large recessed areas, however, two problems may occur. The slip in these areas may separate from the edges of the incised clay around it and may crack as the tile dries or is fired. Both problems result from the different shrinkage rates and moisture content of the slip and the clay body. Either stick with narrow incised lines, cross-hatching, and notching (the effect of shrinkage in these smaller areas is minimal), or engage in some extensive testing.

Once the tile has been biscuit fired, you may wish to coat it with a clear glaze. Alternatively, if you'd rather that

the surface of your tile is not shiny, be sure to fire the tile up to or close to its vitrification point in order to make it strong and water resistant.

SGRAFFITO

Sgraffito, another method of decoration for unfired tiles, makes use of either underglazes (applied to leatherhard or bone-dry tiles) or clay slip (applied to relatively moist tiles). In this technique, the tile is first painted with one or more layers of coloured slips or underglazes. After the coats have dried, the design is cut or scraped through the layers with a potter's needle, craft knife or trimming tool to reveal the clay body underneath (Photo 51). Other tools can be used, of course; just experiment to find the one that's best suited to your design.

Underglazes, which are thinner than slips and which dry very quickly, are best for fine-lined sgraffito designs; clay

Lynda Curtis
Yirkalla. 1993
Image: 22½x19in (57.2x48.3cm)
PHOTOGRAPH BY BOBBY HANSSON

Lynda Curtis
The Elephant Dance. 1992
Image: 4x12in (10.2x30.5cm)
PHOTOGRAPH BY VAN BLERCK PHOTOGRAPHY

Left: Tamara Jaeger
Super Woman. 1991
6x6in (15.2x15.2cm)
PHOTOGRAPH BY CHAS KRIDER

Below: Cairo Cocalis
Reptile Jungle
Each 6x6in (15.2x15.2cm)
PHOTOGRAPH BY ELIZABETH VANDERKOOY

Paula Camenzind
Untitled. 1992
Each 15½x6½in
(39.4x16.5cm)
PHOTOGRAPH BY CARLOS ALEJANDRO

slips tend to be too thick for use when designs are highly detailed. When using underglazes, apply two thin coats of each colour. (Because underglazes dry quickly, you will probably be able to complete this task and transfer your design onto the tile in a single day.) Though underglazes do not need to be matched for fit, slips do.

For the boldest sgraffito look, use only one colour of slip or underglaze, a colour that will contrast with the clay body once the design has been carved. For a more subtle but very beautiful effect, apply several layers of different coloured slips. When you cut the design through the layered colours, the edge of each cut will offer a rainbow effect.

To transfer your design to the underglaze- or slip-covered surface, first place the tile on a turntable. Then rest the design paper (face up) on top of the tile, taping the paper to the table to keep it secure. Trace the design onto the tile by pressing firmly on the design lines with a potter's needle or blunt pencil. The needle or pencil will mark the underglaze or slip underneath without piercing the paper. To transfer very simple designs, just use a pencil to draw the design directly onto the underglaze or slip.

SHELLAC RESIST

Shellac resist is a technique borrowed from print-making. The shellac is applied to specific design areas on an unfired tile, one with or without underglazes or slips on it. (Wax, polyurethane, or oil-based inks can also be used, though shellac seems to work best.) Once it has dried, the shellac acts as a waterproof resist, protecting the areas that it covers. The exposed areas of the tile are then etched away by gently rubbing the entire tile surface with a dampened sponge. Because the unprotected part of the tile's surface is eroded away and is rough in appearance, shellac-resist tiles tend to have a primitive look. This technique therefore lends itself to designs of an organic nature and to ancient motifs.

Shellac can be purchased at a hardware shop. Also buy some denatured alcohol with which to clean your brushes;

neither turpentine nor water will work. If your tile has no slip or underglaze on it, make sure that the tile surface is smooth so that the finished tile will provide an interesting contrast between the textures of smooth and eroded areas. To remove the rolled-out canvas texture, run the flat side of your rubber rib over the tile while the clay is still moist.

Then transfer the design to your bone-dry or leatherhard tile. Next, in a well-ventilated work space or out of doors, paint the shellac onto the areas of your design that you'd like to protect. Shellac, incidentally, can be used straight from the can. In fact, as the alcohol in it evaporates, the shellac will get thicker and will be easier to apply. If it gets too thick, just thin it with some of the alcohol.

For best results, apply the shellac to a bone-dry tile or to one at the advanced leatherhard stage; the bone-dry stage is preferable. Shellac applied to a moist tile may buckle and peel off as the tile dries and shrinks. In addition, the shellac won't be absorbed as quickly by moist clay; painting thin lines will be difficult because the shellac will flow and spread.

After painting on your design, wait until the shellac is dry to the touch before you proceed. (Alcohol-based shellac actually dries quite quickly.) For even better results, allow the shellac to dry for a couple of hours or overnight. Then rub the entire tile surface gently with a damp sponge to erode the unprotected surface areas. (If you've applied the shellac to a bone-dry tile, you can sponge off the surface at any later date, but if the tile is leatherhard, complete the rubbing process shortly after the shellac dries.)

During the biscuit firing, the shellac will burn away, leaving a surface of low, flat relief and strong contrasts between smooth and rough textures. All shellac-covered design areas will be smooth and the same height as the original tile surface. The areas that you've rubbed with the sponge will be recessed, and because the clay body's grog is now exposed, these eroded surfaces will also have a grainy, sand-like texture.

Bobby Hansson
Donna Maria – Vamping.
1976
6x6in (15.2x15.2cm)
PHOTOGRAPH BY BOBBY HANSSON

Bobby Hansson
Carrie Nation. 1976
6x6in
(15.2x15.2cm)
PHOTOGRAPH BY BOBBY HANSSON

A variation on the basic technique is shown in Photos 52 and 53. First apply a coat of coloured slip or underglaze slip to the entire tile surface and then let it dry. On bone-dry ware, drying won't take long; on a leatherhard tile, it may take one or two hours. Then apply the shellac. After the tile is sponged, the areas that were protected by the shellac resist will be the colour of the slip; they'll also be smooth and above the recessed, textured surface of the background clay body (see *Butterfly* tile on page 63).

You can also use the oil-based printer's ink as a resist by applying it through a screen as in screen printing (see the next section) and then wiping the design areas.

SCREEN PRINTING ON TILES

Screen printing, which can be done on either green ware or biscuit, is a sophisticated method of stencilling and is a technique with two advantages for the tile maker. The

technique makes it possible both to transfer an exact image (of either a sketch or a photograph) onto a tile

and to print this exact image on tiles as many times as desired.

The basic procedure entails using a squeegee to pull an underglaze over the open areas of the screen, leaving an even deposit of underglaze on the tile. The tile can then be glazed or left unglazed. Whether you print on biscuit or green ware, the tile must be fired after printing.

First, take your photograph or sketch to a copying service and have a *separation* made; this is a copy of the image that has been shot onto acetate. If your artwork is black and white, with no grey tones or shadows, ask to have it shot as *line art*, which is generally easiest to print on tiles. Artwork with grey tones and shadows, on the other hand, needs to be shot as a *halftone*; this consists of tiny dots, as in a newspaper photograph. In order to print easily, the halftone dots have to be large. Ask the copy shop to shoot halftone images at thirty dots per inch (11.8 per cm). This is double the usual size for printing; the shop may need to blow up an intermediate negative to get dots this large. You, in turn, may have to insist that you know what you're talking about when you make this request – it's an unusual one!

Robert Stratton and Sandra McLean
Detail of *Maya* (right). 1992

Robert Stratton and Sandra McClean
Maya. 1992
69x72in (175.3x182.9cm)

It's also possible to make your own separation, using an opaque black pen or a black oil crayon, by drawing directly on 'prepared' acetate, which can be purchased at any art materials shop. Nuances obtained with the black oil crayons transfer quite well onto the screen.

Once you have your separation, take it to your screen printer and ask them to shoot it onto the screen for you. If you have difficulty finding a copy shop to make a separation, the screen printer can do this, too.

At this point, you'll be ordering a screen and purchasing a squeegee. The squeegee should be 3in (7.6cm) larger than your tile in each dimension and should also be at least 2in (5.1cm) smaller than the inside dimensions of your screen. For a 4x4in (10.2x10.2cm) tile, for example, you'll need a 7in (17.8cm) squeegee.

Purchase a screen that's at least 8in (20.3cm) larger in each dimension than the tile that you plan to print. For a 4x4in (10.2x10.2cm) tile, buy a screen that is 12x12in (30.5x30.5cm) or larger. The screen mesh should be fairly coarse (12XX, 14XX or 16XX), especially if you're a beginner. The higher the mesh number, the finer the mesh will be. The finer the mesh, the more detailed the image, but dried underglaze will also clog finer screens more rapidly than coarse ones. Screens with coarser mesh hold less detail but will deposit more underglaze.

The screen printers will build the screen to your exact size and mesh specifications. To save money, get a screen that is large enough to have several images shot onto it. The cost of one large screen is significantly less than the cost of several small ones. A screen can be re-used many times; just ask a screen printer to put a new image on it.

If you have access to a studio where you can shoot the screen yourself, by all means do so. There are kits available for home shooting, but they're expensive, and we can't recommend them.

Printing on tiles should be executed with commercial underglazes. The consistency of your underglaze is very important; it should be about as thick as standard white glue. Underglaze that's used straight out of the jar is likely to be too thin; it will run underneath the stencil and cause the image to bleed. To thicken it, leave the jar lid off for a few hours. If it's too thick, it may clog the stencil, but too thick is better than too thin.

It's possible to print on both handmade and commercial tiles. Commercial tiles are certainly easier to handle because their surfaces tend to be perfectly flat. They're also uniform in size, which makes registration easier. Handmade tiles, on the other hand, are never perfectly flat or uniform in size; therein lies their beauty. If you do use tiles that you've made yourself, smooth them out as much as possible. The more detailed your image, the flatter your tile needs to be. Even the indentations left by the canvas will inhibit printing. To create a smooth surface, try sponge-brushing your tiles with slip. Line work is probably best for handmade tiles because halftone dots may not print well on tiles that aren't perfectly flat.

Two printing methods are possible. The simplest way to print is unfortunately somewhat inefficient; it necessitates cleaning the screen each time you print a tile. Rest the screen on strips of wood so that the fabric is positioned about 1/2in (1.3cm) away from the tile. Then surround your tile with extra tiles; doing so will provide a smooth transition for your squeegee as it moves across and off the tile that you're printing.

Look through the screen, pushing down on it so that you can see better, and align the stencil (or image) with the tile. Ask someone to hold the screen frame firmly. Next, pour a bead of underglaze across the top of the screen, one slightly longer than the tile itself. Then pull the squeegee across the screen while pressing the screen against the tile (Photo 54). Do this just once, holding the squeegee at a 45° angle and maintaining firm and even pressure on it. As soon as you've made this single pass with the squeegee, the mesh will spring back away from the tile's surface. Lift the screen away carefully to see your printed tile (Photo 55). Clean the screen by running it under cold water and wiping it off with a sponge. Hold it up to the light and make sure that you can see through it.

The second printing method, simultaneously more complicated and more efficient, involves using purchased *screen clamps*, which serve to fasten one edge of the screen to a piece of plywood. The screen can then be swung up and down while you print several tiles – one after another – without shifting the screen's printing position. Before you use the clamped screen, register the exact position in which the tiles will be placed by drawing the tile shape onto your work surface. By placing each tile within this marked outline, you'll ensure that the screen is lowered into the same position on every tile. Several tiles can be

printed before the screen will need to be cleaned.

The screen-printing process requires practice, so don't get discouraged. Save tiles by practising on paper instead. Just cut some newsprint to the size of your actual tiles and place a sheet on top of a tile that's ready to print. Keep practising on one sheet of newsprint after another, until you're ready to print on the actual tile. If you run into problems, the suggestions that follow may help to solve them.

Only parts of the image are printing:
- The underglaze has dried on the screen. Wash the screen, dry it with a towel and try again.
- You don't have enough underglaze on the screen. Same solution as above.
- You aren't applying enough pressure to the squeegee. Try again on a different tile.
- The tile isn't flat. Select a flatter tile and try again.

A vertical line appears across the image on the tile:
- Dried underglaze has stuck to the squeegee. Wash the squeegee and try again.
- There may be a nick in the squeegee. Use the other side of the squeegee on a new tile.

The image is bleeding:
- The underglaze is too thin. Let the underglaze thicken in the open air and try again on another tile.
- You are holding the squeegee at too sharp an angle. Try again on another tile.

CHAPTER EIGHT

FIRING TO HARDNESS

Bonnie Johnson
She Wants to Learn to Dance. 1986
30½x21x6in (77.5x53.3x15.2cm)
PHOTOGRAPH BY STEVE duFOUR

Marcia Hovland
Untitled. 1993
Each 4x4in (10.2x10.2cm)
PHOTOGRAPH BY DENIS DESANDRE

BISCUIT FIRING

Unfired, dried clay that is placed in water will disintegrate and turn back into moist clay. With the application of sufficient heat, however, your clay tile will undergo an irreversible chemical change (known as the *ceramic change*) and will turn into a stone-like material that is no longer water soluble.

Biscuit firing, the first firing that your tile will undergo, hardens the tile and makes it easier to handle when you glaze it. It also allows gases in the clay to escape before the clay is covered with an impervious glaze. If your tile warps or cracks during the biscuit firing, you needn't bother to glaze it and fire it again; just discard it.

There will always be some chemically bound moisture in your unfired tiles – moisture that's related to atmospheric humidity and pressure – but the tiles must be bone dry before they're loaded into the kiln. If the tile is fired before most of this moisture has had a chance to evaporate, the moisture will turn to steam, and as it tries to escape, will cause the tile to crack or explode.

A standard biscuit-firing temperature, no matter what kind of clay you're using, is about 1841°F (1005°C) but may be lower or higher to accommodate particular glazing techniques. If, for instance, you wanted an especially strong tile with a low-fire glaze, you might biscuit fire the tile at 1922°F (1050°C) – a higher temperature than standard – for strength, and then fire the glaze at a temperature that would actually be lower than the biscuit-firing temperature. Different temperatures affect the application of glazes onto your tiles.

Don't biscuit fire at temperatures that are too high. As a clay approaches final vitrification, it gets less and less porous, and glazes won't adhere to non-porous surfaces. Don't fire at too low a temperature (below 1418°F/770°C) either, or the firing won't burn out all the carbon in the clay.

THE STAGES OF FIRING

A general knowledge of the physical and chemical changes that clay goes through during the firing process will help you to attain more successful firings.

The first stage of the slow heating that is required during biscuit firing is called *water smoking* and may take one to several hours depending on the amount of moisture in the tiles, the size and thickness of each tile, and the number of tiles in the kiln. If all the moisture has not escaped by the time the temperature in the kiln has reached 212°F (100°C), then that moisture will turn to steam, which in turn may cause the clay to pop or shatter. For this reason, it's important to keep the firing temperatures from rising too rapidly at this stage; the steam must have time to escape.

As the temperature gradually rises to about 200°C (392°F), any vegetable matter in the clay breaks down and then decomposes. At 573°C (1063°F), an actual chemical change called *quartz inversion* takes place. At this stage, the clay becomes irreversibly hard.

From about 1292°F to 1652°F (700°C to 900°C), the clay's carbon and sulphur burn away and escape as gas. If you heat your tiles too quickly, the clay pores will start to close before these gases escape, and the gases will either form bubbles under the clay's non-porous surface or will cause the tile to bloat during subsequent firings. At this temperature range, if you look through the peepholes in the kiln, you'll see that the kiln's interior is a dull red. Bloating may not be apparent in the biscuit but may appear during the glaze firing as the trapped carbon tries to escape. This carbon will appear as a dark core on the inside of a broken piece of biscuit ware. Once all the carbon is gone, biscuit firing is complete; the biscuit-fired tile is irreversibly hard.

Vitrification, the final stage of firing clay to maturity, is the stage at which the clay becomes completely non-

Geoffrey Meek
Babylonian Lion of the Great Processional Way. 1987
43x103in (109.2x261.6cm)

porous and glass-like – the point just before the clay loses structure and starts to melt. The temperature at which this stage starts can vary greatly with different clay bodies, but usually begins around 1472°F (800°C). If a given clay is fired to a temperature higher than that required for vitrification, the clay will deform and melt into a glass-like state.

Kiln temperatures during biscuit firing should not rise to those required for vitrification because the clay becomes less porous as the body becomes glassier. Clay fired to the biscuit stage is still porous enough to allow liquid glaze to seep in and adhere to the surface of the tile. The subsequent glaze firing (see chapter 10) will bond the glaze to the clay, forming a waterproof, protective coating for your tiles.

BISCUIT-FIRING SCHEDULE
The typical firing schedule that follows, for a 1841°F to 1922°F (1050°C to 1065°C), Orton standard cone 06 to cone 04 biscuit firing in either a 7 cu. ft (.196 cu. m) electric kiln or a .6 cu. ft (.017 cu. m) electric test kiln, illustrates how biscuit firing proceeds, but keep in mind

56

that kilns vary widely. Follow the manufacturer's instructions carefully.

First, load your bone-dry tiles into the kiln, utilizing the available kiln furniture and space as efficiently as possible. By staggering the shelves in a way that permits the heat to circulate, it's possible to compensate for uneven heating within the kiln.

Small and medium-sized tiles, even ones that have been decorated with underglazes, can usually be stacked or leaned vertically against each other (Photo 56) for biscuit firing. Underglazes don't become sticky during firing and won't cause the tiles to stick together.

Following are some suggested stacking heights for tiles of different sizes.

4x4x¼in (10.2x10.2x.6cm)	Three to four tiles high
6x6x½in (15.2x15.2x.1.3cm)	Two to three tiles high
12x12x¾in to 1in (30.5x30.5x1.9cm to 2.5cm)	Rest tiles flat on shelves

Unless they are well supported on flat surfaces, tiles made with certain clays – those with lower vitrification points – may *slump* (or bend) during the biscuit-firing process. Big, thick tiles, even those made with stoneware clays, should also be supported on a level surface. Some grog sprinkled on the shelf under a large tile will help the tile to shrink without stress.

As you arrange your kiln furniture, leave space between the shelves to allow the heat to circulate; about 3in to 4in (7.6cm to 10.2cm) over larger, thicker tiles will do.

Because the backs of stacked tiles aren't exposed to as much airflow as their sides, bloating can be a problem when you fire tiles. If you're accustomed to firing free-standing pottery, you'll need to slow down your firing schedule

Karen Koblitz
Bienveneda Still Life. 1988
36x60x7in (91.4x152.4x17.8cm)
PHOTOGRAPH BY SUSAN EINSTEIN

during the burning-out stage in order to compensate for the different way in which tiles are arranged in a kiln.

Insert the correct pyrometric cone into the kiln-sitter mechanism, selecting the cone to match the firing range you've chosen. For a standard biscuit firing, you might use a cone 05. Keep in mind that the actual temperature in the kiln will often be one cone lower than the cone placed in the sitter.

It's always a good idea to place cone packs in several locations inside the kiln to indicate the actual temperature in each area. Though you won't be able to see all these packs through the peepholes, a study of the cones after the firing is completed will reveal the temperatures that were reached at those locations.

Cone packs are made from the same clay as your tiles and should contain some grog. Each pack also has holes pierced through it. The grog and holes will prevent the pack from exploding during the firing. Form a bowl-like depression in your cone pack to catch the melting cone material before it can drip onto your tiles.

Stick three cones into each pack, placing each cone at a slight angle. The first cone should be one that will bend at the lower end of the firing range to which you plan to fire your clay tile – cone 06 for a standard biscuit firing. The middle cone – cone 05, for example – should reflect the temperature to which you want to fire your tile. And the final cone should be at the upper end of the firing range – cone 04. The kiln will be turned off when the middle cone in the pack has bent over. At that point, the first cone to have melted will probably be completely flat, and the remaining cone will still be upright.

Once the cone packs are in place, set the timer on the kiln for about twelve to thirteen hours and set the temperature control on low for two hours. Different kilns will have different temperature-control arrangements; be sure to read and follow the manufacturer's instructions. Small electric kilns may have only two heating coils, one at the top and one at the bottom, with a switch that turns on one or both. Larger kilns, on the other hand, may have three or four separate dials, each of which controls a section of the kiln's interior.

Open all the peepholes in the kiln, and unless your kiln has a built-in arm for this purpose, use a brick or piece of kiln furniture to prop the lid open by about 2in (5.1cm). Propping the lid open during the early stages of firing will prevent the kiln heating too quickly and will allow the moisture and gases to escape.

After firing the kiln at low for two hours, set the temperature control at medium and continue the firing for another two hours.

Then turn the temperature control to high. If you're using a small electric test kiln leave the one peephole in it open, but on larger kilns close the peepholes at the bottom. Close the kiln lid and readjust the timer for about six to eight hours.

Either the kiln sitter (if the kiln has one) or the automatic timer will shut off the kiln – whichever mechanism is activated first. (The kiln will shut off automatically when the cone in the sitter melts. The automatic timer shuts off the kiln when the timer runs out.) Keep an eye on the cone pack. If the cone 05 in it melts before the kiln shuts off automatically, turn the kiln off manually.

Before opening the door or closed peepholes, allow your tiles to cool in the kiln for at least ten hours. The flat planes of tiles are not as structurally sound as the curved spheres of fired pottery, so tiles are more susceptible to cracking from thermal shock. After ten hours have passed, you can open the peepholes and lift the lid by 2in (5.1cm), but don't open the lid completely or remove the tiles for another two to three hours. Take out the tiles once they're cool to the touch.

Chapter Nine

Surface Decoration on Biscuit-Fired Tiles

Kenneth Dierck
Starry Night. 1992
15x15x¼in (38.1x38.1x.6cm)
PHOTOGRAPH BY JOHN EISELEIN

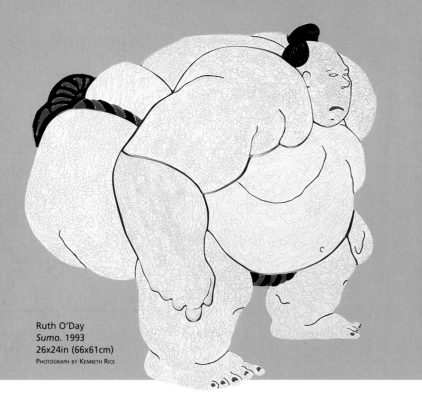

Ruth O'Day
Sumo. 1993
26x24in (66x61cm)

Frank Giorgini
Lizard. 1991
6x6in (15.2x15.2cm)

GLAZES

Glazes, which contain more fluxing material than underglazes, melt and fuse onto the surface of a tile when the tile is fired, providing a hygienic, non-porous, waterproof coating that can be clear or colourful, shiny or matt, smooth or textured. Unlike underglazes, they actually seep into the tile and form a glass-like bond right down to the clay itself. As a general rule, glazes are not applied to green ware.

Available from your clay supplier, glazes come in 2oz (56.7g), 4oz (113.4g) and 1pt (568ml) jars, in a wide range of colours. In contrast to underglazes, however, their colours in the bottle often bear no relationship to their fired colours. This can make application a mystery. Your supplier is likely to have a glazed-colour guide consisting of glazed and fired clay buttons. You'll find this guide very helpful when you select glaze colours.

Glazes can be formulated from dry, powdered ingredients – clays, frits, oxides and others – but the process is hazardous to health and is not recommended for beginners. (For experts, some glaze formulas can be found in Appendix D on page 138.) Besides being potentially dangerous, glaze formulation requires the use of specialized equipment and working conditions. To learn about glaze chemistry, a science in itself, enrol in a local pottery course where you'll have access both to the chemicals and to a safe working environment.

Commercial glazes for firing at 1841°F (1005°C) to 1922°F (1050°C) in an electric kiln is usually the most accessible method available for glaze firing. Other methods of glaze firing, including stoneware, reduction, raku, salt and saggar, require equipment and techniques too specialized for inclusion in this book, but brief descriptions of each are given in the next chapter.

As your work progresses, you'll no doubt wish to experiment with more unique glaze surfaces than are yielded by commercially available glazes, as well as with different firing techniques. Use of pre-mixed commercial glazes, however, is definitely the easier way to start.

It's not uncommon to work long and hard to create a unique hand-pressed relief tile, only to have it look gaudy and cheap because of an inappropriate commercial glaze choice. Your selection of glazes will depend upon a number of factors; an understanding of these will help you to make wise choices.

As explained in chapter 2, the kiln that you'll be using may limit your choice of glazes. Some glazes are made for oxidation firing; others must be reduction fired. Certain stoneware glazes, which require firing temperatures up to 2300°F (1260°C), just won't work in a small electric kiln.

Another factor that will influence your choice of glaze will be what you want your tile to look like. In general, shiny, colourful results are associated with low-fire glazes or with low-fire underglazes covered with a clear glaze. For earthy colours with a mottled, breaking effect, choose higher-temperature stoneware colours such as those in my *Lizard* tile (shown above).

As you gain experience with glazes, you will develop your own glaze-application techniques, as well as preferences for certain manufacturers' brands of glaze colours.

The most common methods of glaze application on biscuit are brushing, dipping and spraying, although spraying is usually done with underglazes. Glazes, like underglazes, can be thinned with water to the proper consistency for each method. Stir your glaze before you use it, as some ingredients tend to settle at the bottom. If the glaze has dried out, just add water before stirring. Also make sure that your tile is free of dust and oils; rinse it in water and let it dry until the little puddles of water on the surface disappear.

Kenneth Dierck
Bird Watcher. 1991
31x30½x⅝in (78.7x77.5x1.6cm)
<small>PHOTOGRAPH BY JOHN EISELEIN</small>

Susan Grossman
Untitled. 1991
6x6in (15.2x15.2cm)
<small>PHOTOGRAPH BY SUSAN GROSSMAN</small>

PAINTING WITH GLAZES

Designs that are painted with glazes will yield entirely different results from those that are painted with under-glazes. Commercial low-fire glazes on a biscuit surface will produce bright colours, but the edges where two colours meet will flow and meld together during the subsequent glaze firing. Of course, you may be aiming for this effect.

To paint with glazes, use soft brushes in sizes compatible with your design. Most commercial glazes are applied in two or three even coats, and time is allowed for each coat to dry before the next is applied. Do check instructions on the glaze container before you start, but feel free to experiment by mixing colours, too. Keep in mind that the edges where two colours touch or overlap will form a third, blended colour.

Majolica glaze is especially versatile. Now formulated without tin because of the dangers of metallic oxides, majolica is a low-fire glaze and is usually a creamy, translucent white. It makes a good base glaze over which coloured stains and oxides can be brushed. The stains and oxides sink and blend into the glaze surface during the glaze firing, providing a painted effect. Majolica can also be applied with other glazes or applied under or over underglazes.

No matter which glaze application technique you choose, you must be sure not to apply glaze to the back surface of your tile. If you're brushing the glaze on, cover only the top surface and leave an unglazed area about ⅛in to ¼in (.3cm to .6cm) wide along the bottom of the tile's edge. Glaze that completely covers the edges or that covers the bottom will melt in the firing and will fuse your tile right onto the kiln shelf. To remove the tile – a very unpleasant task – you'd have to use a hammer, chisel and grinder.

WAX RESIST FOR GLAZE SEPARATION

To keep glaze colours from blending into one another in fine-lined designs, try the *wax-resist* technique. In this technique, a fine line of wax resist is painted between the design areas before glazing colours are applied. The wax burns off in the firing, leaving a narrow, dry area of bare tile visible between the glaze colours. This is a variation of a traditional resist technique called *cuerda seca* (see page 10) and is very effective with terracotta tiles; the warm terracotta colour that appears between the glaze colours is especially attractive.

By mixing colours with the wax resist, it's possible to apply colours to the dry lines between glazes, too. When the wax burns away, the oxide colour will remain on the tile.

A similar *cloisonné* effect can be created on tiles pressed out with carved plaster blocks by applying glaze colours between the raised design areas. These raised areas will prevent the colours from blending with each other. Unless you paint these surfaces with an underglaze first, they'll remain the colour of your clay.

DIPPING WITH GLAZES

Dipping biscuit tiles into glazes is an application process that produces a very uniform coating. (You wouldn't usually dip green ware into an underglaze; an unfired tile might become muddy if it were dipped, and the process would require more underglaze than you're likely to have on hand.)

Before the tile is dipped, its entire back surface and the bottom portion of its edges must be covered with a wax resist so that the glaze will stick only to the front of the tile. A water-based wax resist is commercially available and is safer to use than hot paraffin. Inexpensive foam

Above: Barbara Grygutis
American Loveseat. 1993
Kenneth Myer Park,
Coconut Grove, Florida
36x72x72in
(91.4x182.9x182.9cm)
PHOTOGRAPH BY BARBARA GRYGUTIS

Left: Barbara Grygutis
Cruising San Mateo 1. 1991
City of Albuquerque
Public Art Collection
264x192x72in
(670.6x487.7x182.9cm)
PHOTOGRAPH BY TIM FULLER

Daniel Oberti
Maquette. 1990
12x26in (30.5x66cm)
PHOTOGRAPH BY DANIEL OBERTI

brushes make excellent applicators for the wax. Either hold the tile in one hand while you brush on the wax with the other (Photo 57), or use a tile-waxing stand to hold the tile while the wax is applied (Photo 58). Instructions for making the tile-waxing stand are given in chapter 14.

Let the wax dry thoroughly. Have on hand enough glaze to cover the tile completely once the tile is submerged. The most efficient container for your glaze is a tall, narrow, or even rectangular bucket that's just wide enough to accommodate the tile.

A *tile dipper* will keep you from getting finger or clamp marks on the tile (Photo 59). See chapter 14 for instructions on how to make one of these useful tools from a wire coat-hanger or scrap wood. Position your tile so that it rests flat on the long arms of the tool and is supported along its bottom edge by the 90° wire ends. Hold the V-shaped end of the tool in your hand while you hold the tile

58

59

57

down with your thumb. Submerge the tile completely in the glaze bucket. You shouldn't get more than the tip of your gloved thumb wet during this process. Because the

Frank Giorgini
Elephant. 1992
12x12in (30.5x30.5cm)
PHOTOGRAPH BY BOBBY HANSSON

Pewabic Pottery
Fireplace Surround. 1988. 51x88x12in (129.5x223.5x30.5cm)
PHOTOGRAPH BY TIM THAYER

tile's back is covered with wax, no clamp or finger marks will be left on its surface.

Lift the tile out of the dip (Photo 60) and shake it slightly to remove some of the excess glaze. Then place the tile (face up) on some newspaper. The glaze will be dry to the touch within half an hour, but make sure that its top

60

surface is totally dry because you will have to handle it.

When the glaze is dry, gently hold the tile upside down with the glazed surface in the palm of your hand and use a damp sponge to remove any beads of glaze from the back. Don't handle the tile any more than necessary at this stage; the unfired glaze may wear off. If this should happen, just dab on a little more with a paintbrush.

The dipping technique works very well with relief tiles. By using a glaze that breaks into different colours as it flows and pools in the different areas of your design, you'll be able to achieve some spectacular results with a single dipping. The finished appearance of these types of breaking glazes can vary greatly depending on the thickness of the application. The glaze colouration will look very natural because you've allowed the breaking qualities of

the glaze and the effects of the firing process to do the work for you.

One way to produce glazed areas that vary in thickness is to pour or dip additional glaze over the tile. Wait for the first coat to dry. Then hold or brace the tile inside a container (Photo 61). Scoop up some glaze with a smaller container and pour it over the front of the tile. The glaze will be thicker wherever the poured application overlaps. With certain glazes, the overlapped areas will also vary in colour on the fired tile.

61

GLAZE SCRAPING

An effective technique used in conjunction with dipping or pouring is to scrape the glaze off certain areas of your design, but unless you're working in a professional studio with excellent ventilation, this method should only be executed out of doors. It works best on tiles with raised, uniformly flat areas, such as those created with the layering technique. The *Elephant* tile shown above was made with this technique.

Dip or pour glaze over the entire front of the tile and let the glaze dry. (It will be workable within half an hour, but

Karen Koblitz
*Raffaellesco Deruta
Lunette.* 1993
23x41½x7in
(58.4x105.4x17.8cm)
SUSAN EINSTEIN

the tile can stand overnight if you like.) Spread out some newspaper on a table, place a turntable on top of the newspaper, and place the tile on top of the turntable. Be sure to put on a dust mask. Then, using a metal rib, scrape off most of the glaze on the raised areas of the tile (Photo 62). Whenever possible, scrape in the direction of the design lines, not perpendicular to them. Spin the turntable for easier access to these lines.

63

62

Next, rub a synthetic scouring pad over the scraped surfaces (Photo 63). Tip and shake the scrapings off the tile onto the newspaper. Don't blow the dust off; gently remove it with a soft brush instead. The finished tile will be glazed in the recessed areas, and the natural colour of the clay will show through wherever you have scraped the glaze away.

A similar effect can be achieved by scraping the tile first and then using a damp sponge instead of a scouring pad. The sponge will pull some of the diluted glaze material across the clay and will leave the clay surfaces a bit shinier and darker than glazed clay that has been scraped and scoured. Using a sponge is also a much less dusty, and therefore safer, process.

SPRAYING WITH GLAZES

Spraying is an efficient way to apply a uniform coating of glaze to your tile. It's also a good way to apply a clear glaze over underglazes painted onto biscuit without smearing the unfired underglaze colours. This technique, however, requires a ventilated spray booth, a proper mask, and spray-gun equipment. In addition, practice is required to prepare glaze of the correct consistency, to adjust the spray pattern and pressure, and to gauge the correct distance from which to spray the tile. It is possible however, to obtain fine results with sprayed underglazes or glazes – results that are comparable to delicate airbrush work with paints.

Note that it's difficult to apply an even coat of sprayed glaze over a relief tile, because the flow of spray over the uneven surface will often leave bare spots. Spraying over stencils on biscuit ware is no different from spraying underglazes over stencils on green ware. When you use a stencil, glazes can also be patted on with a sponge or painted on with a brush.

Joseph A. Triplo
Study for Tile Floor. 1989
33x53in (83.8x134.6cm)
PHOTOGRAPH BY DAVE PALMER

STAINS

Stains are a mixture of water and colouring oxides, the natural materials from which the colours for glazes and underglazes are derived, and can be rubbed, brushed, sponged, or sprayed onto biscuit. They're often applied to accent, recessed, or textured areas; the excess stain is rubbed off with a damp sponge to give an antique effect.

Stains will colour clay whether or not it is glazed and will also affect glazes. They can also be used at all firing ranges but their effects are greater at higher temperatures and in reduction firings. The following list gives some oxides and their general colour effects:

Chromium oxide . . . . Green
Cobalt carbonate . . . . Blue
Copper carbonate . . . . . . Warm grey/brown to green
Iron oxide . . . . Reddish brown to black
Manganese . . . . Black

Beginners should not attempt to mix their own stains as the ingredients can be toxic. Experienced tile makers mix stain in small batches by stirring a couple of teaspoons of oxide into 1pt (568ml) of water to make a thin, watery solution. Stain colourants, which come in a full range of colours, are available commercially in micronized crystal form (coloured powders).

UNDERGLAZES ON BISCUIT

Underglazes may be brushed or sprayed onto biscuit, or sponged down and then off for an antique effect, but remember that your tile may require an additional firing before you coat the underglaze with a glaze, in order to prevent the underglaze colours from smearing. Commercial underglazes for painting are available in a set that resembles a child's watercolour set.

For a marbled effect on biscuit, swirl together two or more underglaze colours in a shallow baking sheet. Then press your biscuit tile (face down) into the mixed colours. Pick up the tile, let it dry, fire it again, apply a clear glaze coating, and finally, glaze fire the marbled tile.

CHAPTER TEN

GLAZE FIRING, OVERGLAZES AND DECALS

Anne Lloyd
Birches. 1993
8x5½in (20.3x14.5cm)
PHOTOGRAPH BY JOHN CARLANO

GLAZE-FIRING TECHNIQUES

During the glaze firing, which is usually the second firing of your tile, the liquid glazes will fuse onto the tile's surface to provide a hygienic, waterproof, protective coating. While underglazes, which consist of clay slip and a small amount of fluxing material, will stick to the tile during biscuit firing, glazes actually melt and fuse with the clay to form a glass-like coating. Note that glaze firing to a given temperature usually proceeds more rapidly than biscuit firing to the same temperature because the chemical changes in the clay have already taken place.

A great many glaze-firing techniques have been perfected over the centuries. The source of heat (electric, gas or solid-fuel kilns), the temperature range of the clay (low fire earthenware or high-fire stoneware, for example), and the firing method (oxidation, reduction, raku, saggar or salt), all yield an endless variety of surface finishes. Brief descriptions of these firing techniques follow, but the most accessible method is probably oxidation firing in an electric kiln. Try the library, a book-shop, or a ceramic supplier for further information on firing methods other than oxidation.

In *raku* firing, a technique that originated in sixteenth-century Japan, glazed or unglazed biscuit or green ware is heated and rapidly cooled. Traditional Japanese tea bowls produced in this manner are extremely heat resistant and can be comfortably held even when their contents are very hot.

Today, the raku technique is used on all types of ceramic objects. Raku kilns, which are often gas fired, are usually located out of doors. The fired ware is removed from the kiln while it's still glowing hot and is placed in a container filled with combustible materials such as leaves, straw, newspaper or sawdust. These materials are ignited by the heat of the ware, and the clay is blackened by the carbon in the heavy smoke that results. Raku-fired glazes often *crackle* (or *craze*); the thermal shock of the ware's rapid cooling creates beautiful, fine-lined cracks in the

glaze, which are sometimes blackened by the carbon produced in this firing technique. Natural lustres often occur on raku glazes.

In *saggar* firing, the ware is placed in a lidded, refractory clay container filled with sawdust or other combustible materials. By creating this small, controlled atmosphere within the kiln, it's possible to affect the clay and the glazes in particular ways. The box also protects the ware from flames or gases. Saggar firing, like raku firing, may create smoke marks on the ware.

Salt firing, originally a German technique, is one in which the glaze is actually created during the firing. By introducing common salt into the kiln fire at certain intervals, soda is produced, which in turn combines with alumina and silica in the clay body to form a glaze on the ware's surface.

GLAZE FIRING

Because your tiles have been biscuit fired, they've already undergone the firing stages of water smoking, vegetable matter decomposition, ceramic change, and carbon and sulphur oxidation. For this reason, the general schedule of temperature rise in a glaze firing is somewhat different.

In the kiln, a slow drying period of low heat will remove any extra moisture in the glaze. The kiln temperature should rise gradually and steadily. At about 1063°F (573°C), a sudden expansion of the biscuit ware takes place, one that's a result of the crystalline silica structure of the clay. The point at which this expansion occurs is called the dunting point, and if the heat rise is rapid during this stage, stress cracks can occur in the tiles.

Up to the original temperature to which you biscuit-fired your tiles, the clay body is unaffected. As the temperature rises and the glaze actually starts to melt, the clay body fuses with the glaze. This fusion (or integration) is what forms a strong glaze layer. At this stage, the glaze melts to glass and adheres permanently to the tile. If you've used the correct cone in the kiln sitter, the kiln

Anne Lloyd
Old-Time Baseball Player. 1993
14x6in (35.6x15.2cm)
PHOTOGRAPH BY JOHN CARLANO

Carol Susan Clemens
Burned Out. 1988
18x24in (45.7x61cm)

Frank Giorgino
*Afro Tile.*1992
12x12in (30.5x30.5cm)
PHOTOGRAPH BY BOBBY HANSSON

Opposite page: Penny Truitt
Outliers II. 1992
18x40in (45.7x101.6cm)
PHOTOGRAPH BY JOHN SCARLATA

should automatically shut off at this glaze maturation point. A back-up safety-timer mechanism that will prevent overfiring is available for most kilns; be sure to get one.

GLAZE-FIRING SCHEDULE

Always follow the kiln manufacturer's instructions for firing. A typical glaze firing for a low-temperature glaze firing – 1841°F (1005°C) to 1922°F (1050°C), standard Orton cone 06 to 04 – might proceed as follows. This schedule is for a 7 cu. ft (.196 cu. m) electric kiln or a .6 cu. ft (.27 cu. m) electric test kiln. For a general high-temperature glaze-firing schedule in a gas kiln, see Appendix E on page 139.

When you load your tiles for a glaze firing, be sure that the backs of the tiles are free of glaze, that the glaze on the tiles is dry, and that the tiles don't touch each other (Photo 64). In its molten state, the glaze will flux and flow and stick to anything that it touches. Try to pack your kiln efficiently, using all available space.

64

Insert a cone 05 or cone 04 in the kiln sitter and set the timer for about ten hours. Then set the temperature control on low for one hour. Leave all the peepholes open and prop the lid open by about 2in (5.1cm), as shown in Photo 65.

65

When the hour has passed, reset the temperature control at medium for another hour, leaving the peepholes and lid as they were.

After that hour has passed, close the lid and all the peepholes except the top one. Set the temperature control at high and readjust the timer for about seven to eight hours. Depending on the volume of tiles within the kiln, it will continue to fire for seven to eight hours.

After the kiln sitter has shut off the kiln, let the kiln cool for at least twelve hours. This cooling-down period, a very important stage of the glaze-firing process, is the period during which the colours of many glazes are set, and it may take twice as long as the actual firing. The kiln should be left

Opposite page:
John Bade
Wave. 1984
48x96x³/₄in
(121.9x243.8
x1.9cm)
PHOTOGRAPH BY PAUL KODAMA

Right: Frank Giorgini
Sunset mural from
fireplace and mural
installation. 1991
30x48in
(76.2x121.9cm)
PHOTOGRAPH BY TOM TEICH

closed so that it will cool naturally. If it cools too rapidly, the glazes may craze, or the tile itself may crack. Note that if you'd like to create crazing on decorative ware, a commercial, clear crackle glaze is available, one that is formulated to crackle during normal cooling in an electric oxidation firing. By applying ink or stain over the cracks, you can create a look similar to raku. When the kiln is sufficiently cool to the touch, open the lid by about 2in (5.1cm).

When the interior has cooled completely, open the lid fully for a first look at your work. Opening a kiln is something like getting a present. Sometimes that present is wonderful – even spectacular – and the experience is exhilarating. At other times, you may wish you could return the gift for something else, but that's the excitement of working in ceramics.

Try to base your initial judgement of your finished tile on its own merits rather than on your expectations. If you don't like what you see, don't refire your tiles right away. Wait a day or two and take another look. You may very well find that your opinion has changed.

After removing your tiles from the kiln, don't stack them on top of one another without providing a cushioning layer of newspaper or cardboard between the layers.

OVERGLAZES

Overglazes – very low temperature glazes that are applied to previously fired glazed surfaces – consist of colouring oxides and frits, usually in an oil medium. Similar to oil paints in consistency, they are brushed on and are fused onto the glazed surface in a separate 1103°F (595°C) to 2030°F (1110°C) firing. This low-firing range melts and fuses the overglazes without melting the previously fired glaze.

Commercially available from your ceramic supplier in a wide range of colours, overglazes are reasonably permanent but are not as durable as higher fired glazes. They do wear off with repeated rubbing and cleaning. Opaque colours are often referred to as *overglaze enamels* and transparent colours as *china paints*. Metallic overglazes, such as gold, silver, platinum and copper are also available. These are quite expensive and are most commonly seen as gold or silver banding on tableware.

A thin metallic film of overglaze that covers the surface of a glaze is referred to as a *lustre*. This thin metallic-oxide coating can be applied to the glazed ware by brush or as a spray, or can be produced on the glazed surface during the firing process through a technique called *fuming*. The result is lustrelike and iridescent.

Decorating with overglazes and lustres should only be undertaken with the greatest of care. Toxic chemicals can be released during both the application and firing processes, so proper masks and ventilation are a must. For health reasons, I do not use lustres and overglazes in the classroom environment.

DECALS

Overglaze designs can also be applied in the form of printed decals. These are transferred by wetting a paper backing material and sliding the image off it, onto the fired glaze surface of your tile. The tile is then refired to 1103°F (595°C) to 1463°F (795°C). Decals may be ordered from certain silk-screening companies' catalogues, which contain hundreds of pre-made images. Black or (much more expensive) full-colour decals can also be made up from your own designs or photographs. Cost is relative to the size of the decal, its colours, and the quantity desired. Be prepared to provide the decal printing company with camera-ready artwork. Decals can be handmade, too, by screen printing them onto special decal paper.

Left: Susan Nowogrodzki
The Life Cycle: Water. 1987–1988
55x38in (139.7x96.5cm)

Lower left: Wickie Lynn Bowman
Cow Skull. 1992
12x12in (30.5x30.5cm)

Below: Penny Truitt
Winter Beach II. 1990
18x22in (45.7x55.9cm)

CHAPTER ELEVEN

MOSAICS

Zuthbeida Lazrek
Mala Madre (Spider Plant). 1986
48x36in (121.9x91.4cm)
PHOTOGRAPH BY Z. QUILES

Diane Winters
Springfield Garden (detail). 1991
22x28in (55.9x71.1cm)

MOSAIC MATERIALS AND COMPOSITION

A *mosaic* is made by arranging pieces of durable materials to compose a permanent design. These materials are sometimes referred to as *tesserae* and include shaped tiles, broken piece of tile, glass and marble. The pieces can be set in cement (a process known as a *mud* job) or fixed to a solid surface with ceramic adhesives. *Grout,* a cement-like material, is used to fill the spaces between the installed tiles.

MOSAIC DESIGN

Basically, there are two ways to compose a mosaic design. Many artists use a 'puzzle' technique, shaping and cutting each tile to fit together with other shaped tiles, just as the pieces of a puzzle or the parts of a stained-glass window are made to fit together. The tiles at the top of this page were made in this manner.

Artists who use this technique must make design decisions as they divide their compositions into individual tile shapes. The *grout lines* (the spaces between the tiles that are later filled with grout) become very important; they provide the linear elements that define or outline objects in the composition. If you were to use this technique to depict a landscape and sky, for example, you might cut some of the tiles into the shapes of mountain peaks and divide the sky into cloud-shaped tiles that would fit around the mountains.

To design and make a mosaic in this way, first make a line drawing of your full-sized design on a piece of large paper. Include and number each individual tile shape in your composition. Next, roll out a slab of clay as large as the composition – if the composition is small – or as large as one section if the composition itself is large. To impress the design lines into the clay, place the design paper on the slab and trace over the lines with a slightly blunted pencil. Remove the paper and cut out the tile shapes.

Rather than calculating shrinkage for grout-line spaces, wait until the tile pieces that you cut from the large slab are leatherhard. The spaces left between the individual pieces once they've dried and are assembled will provide grout lines of roughly the correct size. If you need to make adjustments in order to make the grout lines wider, scrape the leatherhard tiles down so that the spaces between them are uniform.

As soon as you've cut the tile shapes, on the back of each one mark the number that corresponds to that tile's number in the drawing. This will make assembly of the finished tiles much easier. Sandwich the flat tiles between layers of wall-board so that they'll dry flat. Once the tiles are leatherhard, you may have to trim and reshape them.

The other, more traditional approach to making mosaics is to fill up each design element by arranging many shaped or broken pieces of tile. These small tile pieces can be cut from tiles that you have glazed and fired yourself or can be snipped from pieces of commercial tile. Look for damaged tiles at a tile shop; these will come in a wide range of colours and will cost little or nothing. If you choose to glaze your own tiles and then nip pieces from them, you may want to glaze long strips of clay rather than squares or rectangles. The strips are easy to hold in one hand while you nip off small pieces with the other.

Always wear safety glasses and thick gloves when snipping up tiles and use a good-quality pair of *tile nippers*. Snipping with this sharp-jawed tool, which is similar to a pair of pliers, isn't easy, but with practice, you'll soon have buckets of categorized tile pieces with which to work. As you polish your nipping skills, keep in mind that traditional Islamic mosaic artisans cut the tiles with a chisel and hammer. In fact, skilled artisans specialize in cutting

Above and left: George F. Fishman
Faces of Flower Avenue. 1991
114x36in dia. (289.6x91.4cm dia.)

Below: Nancy McCroskey
Aerial Rhythm. 1989
72x144x6in (182.9x365.8x15.2cm)
Photograph by Bill Mills

John Bade
Mother and Child. 1986
48x48x1¼in (121.9x121.9x3.2cm)
PHOTOGRAPH BY PAUL KODAMA

Beth Katleman
Fallen Leaf Table (detail). 1992
30x42x26in
(76.2x106.7x66cm)
PHOTOGRAPH BY WILLIAM RIVELLI

certain shapes, while the artist simply fills in the design by selecting from among the shapes made for him.

MOSAIC ASSEMBLY AND INSTALLATION

Modern materials have provided the mosaic artist with some new tricks of the trade – here's one of them. First, purchase two grades of clear plastic adhesive film, one sticky and the other not very sticky (the 'contact' paper sold in many hardware shops will do). Next, draw your design on a piece of paper and secure it to the table. Tack down a large piece of the less sticky film over your drawing, with the sticky side facing up. Arrange and fill in all the areas of your design by pressing the tile pieces onto the sticky paper; your design will show clearly through it. This film will keep your small mosaic pieces from sliding around if you bump the table as you work.

After you've completed the mosaic design, lay the stickier sheet of film face down on top of the tile pieces. Your tiles will now be sandwiched between the two layers, and you can transport them to the installation site without disturbing their positions.

To mount this sandwiched design, first turn the sandwich over so that the bottoms of the tiles face up. Then peel off the layer of less sticky film, which is now on top. Coat the back of the mosaic and the mounting surface with adhesive (see chapter 13). Lift the mosaic up by gripping the paper

beneath it and position its back against the mounting surface. As you do, the sticky film will continue to hold the mosaic pieces together. When the mosaic is in place, beat it smooth and flat against the mounting surface. When the adhesive has set, peel off the plastic film and apply grout.

If your design is large, you'll need to assemble and install the mosaic in manageable sections – perhaps 1x2ft (30.5x61.0cm) in size. Smaller mosaics of uniform thickness may be arranged on sheets of perforated paper, which are made for the tile industry in a variety of sizes – 1x2ft (30.5x61.0cm), for example. Apply spray adhesive to one surface of the paper and arrange your mosaic pieces face up on the sticky surface. Coat the mounting surface with tile adhesive, and then press the mosaic, paper side down, directly against the mounting surface. The tile adhesive will spread through the perforations to the backs of the tile pieces.

For information on installation tools and adhesives, see chapter 13.

CHAPTER TWELVE

TILE DESIGN

Mimi Strang
Window Box. 1990
37x37x2in (94x94x5.1cm)

Above: Shel Neymark
Wildlife of the Rio Grande Window. 1991
60x42x9in (152.4x106.7x22.9cm)
PHOTOGRAPH BY HERB LOTZ

Above left: Shel Neymark
Datura Fireplace. 1991
38x45in (96.5x114.3cm)
PHOTOGRAPH BY HERB LOTZ

Below: Judith Williams
Flood Control Wall. 1989
72inx800ft (182.9cmx243.8m)

Beth Starbuck
and Steven Goldner
Tile Table. 1988
25x40x20in
(63.5x101.6x50.8cm)

DESIGNING FOR APPLICATION

As you've probably realized by now, there are may ways to transform your ideas into finished tiles. Some of these have been explained to you, but now that you have a place from which to start, be inventive and develop some of your own. Your knowledge and craftsmanship will improve with experience.

Start with modest projects: a tabletop, tray, backsplash, or countertop. You'll learn most from your mistakes, and the many technical steps that make up the ceramic process leave plenty of room for those! Don't be discouraged. The rewards of success will outweigh the disappointments.

By identifying the design parameters before you begin a project, you'll improve your chances for success. Begin by asking yourself what function your tiles will serve. Will they be decorative or will they provide a waterproof, hygienic surface covering as well? Will they be installed indoors or out? Will they be in an environment that's always wet, such as a swimming pool, fountain or shower? Will they be installed on the floor or wall?

The answers to these questions will help you to determine how hard and porous your clay needs to be and what sort of glaze to use on it. The ceramic industry has developed a standard code for rating the porosity and hardness of tiles in relation to their intended use. For a fee, the British Ceramic Research Institute (see page 142) will test a sample tile.

Some function-based guidelines follow to help you make design choices. Once you've decided on a flat or relief design, you may apply any one (or a combination) of the surface decoration techniques that you've learned – inlay, shellac resist, or sgraffito, for example.

TABLETOPS, COUNTERTOPS, AND BACKSPLASHES

Design type: Flat on countertops; low relief on backsplashes.

Glazes and firing: Glazes necessary for hygiene, stain resistance, and ease of cleaning. Low-fire glazes adequate, but biscuit recommended. Stoneware clays and glazes are even better.

FIREPLACES AND MURALS

Design type: Flat, low relief, or high relief.

Glazes and firing: Glazes optional (probably unnecessary as a moisture barrier). Low-fire glazes adequate. Use biscuit 2075°F (1135°C) for fireplaces because heavy objects such as wood and hearth tools may damage clay that's fired at lower temperatures. Stoneware clays and glazes are even better.

WALLS IN DRY AREAS

Design type: Flat, low relief, or high relief as accents.

Glazes and firing: Low-fire glazes adequate. Stoneware clays and glazes are even better.

WALLS IN WET AREAS (SHOWERS, POOLS AND FOUNTAINS)

Design type: Flat, low-relief tiles. High-relief tiles appropriate only when they won't prove hazardous upon bodily contact.

Glazes and firing: Glazed, low-fire clays adequate if vitreous. Stoneware clays and glazes are even better. Tile surfaces must be sealed against moisture with a glaze, and the clay body must be fired to vitrification. Sealers for the grout are available, but the less porous the clay body, the better.

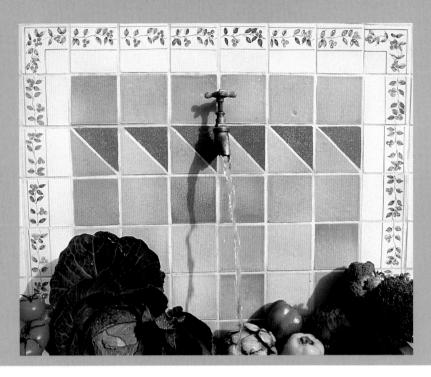

Fired Earth Tiles
Provencal: Vert Ocean and Cinnamon with Cerise Border. Ongoing
Each 3⁹/₁₆x3⁹/₁₆x⁵/₁₆in
(9x9x.8cm)

FLOORS

Design type: Flat tiles; flat, low-relief tiles.

Glazes and firing: Durability is important. The higher fired, stronger and denser the clay, the better. Minimum temperature of 2075°F (1135°C) recommended. (Low-fire earthenware tiles, such as Mexican terracotta, create a warm, rustic look but chip easily and are so porous that they must be sealed with waxes, oils or chemicals. They also require regular maintenance.) Use matt or textured glazes; shiny ones may be too slippery, especially when wet. Encaustic tiles are a traditional choice.

TILE DESIGNS

The first thing to consider when you're designing with tiles is that they may be around for a long time. Tiles are relatively expensive to make or to purchase, and once they're installed, they are difficult and expensive to remove. Create designs that are more than momentarily appealing, ones that will fit comfortably in their environment for years to come. Well-made and properly installed tiles can last for hundreds of years, so design for the long term, not for the short. If your tiles are too bizarre or trendy, you or your client will soon tire of them.

Tile sizes should match the scale of your environment. In general, the larger the room, the larger the tile. There are always exceptions to this rule, however; it's up to you to decide what tile size to use in a given space. Of course, you can create a pattern that has overall interest by working with various tile sizes and shapes.

More is not necessarily better. If you've created a boldly designed tile for a wall, pressing out hundreds of them to cover the entire wall area would probably be disastrous. The endless repetition of the individual tile design would diminish its visual impact.

A better way to highlight a special tile might be to feature it at pre-selected locations on the wall and surround it with flat background tiles. The unique tile, in this example, is referred to as an *accent tile,* and the surrounding background tiles are called *field tiles.* An accent tile that fits well in both size and colour with less expensive, commercially available field tiles is a very desirable product. And clients will probably be more willing to pay for expensive tiles when only a few are necessary to create a custom-made look for the total architectural environment.

Try to offer something unique in your designs and surface treatment. A great many beautiful and flawlessly made commercial tiles are already available. As an individual tile artist, you must therefore try to capitalize on your own talents – the creativity of your mind and the work of your hands. Add to that the love from your heart, and you will produce tiles that are objects of beauty for generations to come.

COMPUTER TILE DESIGN

If tile design becomes more than a part-time interest for you and you own a home computer, you may want to consider purchasing computer design software. Once you've

66

Elizabeth Grajales
Snow Leopard (from the PS 92 Project,
Who Else Shares Our World). 1992
8x8in (20.3x20.3cm)

Frank D'Amico
Untitled. 1993
11x12in (27.9x30.5cm)
PHOTOGRAPH BY FRANK D'AMICO

installed this software, you'll have a graphics tool that lends itself extremely well to tile design (Photo 66).

There are many advantages to using a computer for design purposes. The most important is that you'll save a great deal of time that would otherwise be spent drawing and redrawing designs by hand or running back and forth to a photocopying shop. A design program will allow you to create repeats, alternative design shapes and design variations. It will also help you to re-size design elements quickly, store them in a permanent 'library', and combine

or change them as you choose (Photo 67).

Your first step will be to select software for your home computer. Before you set off to do this, answer the following questions.

- *Is your computer a Macintosh, IBM, or IBM compatible?* You must know this because software is system specific. If you own an IBM or compatible, what size disks and drive do you use? IBM software is available on either 5.25in (13.3cm) or 3.5in (8.9cm)

floppy disks. Macintosh software is available on 3.5in (8.9cm) floppy disks and on CD-ROM.

- *How much available RAM (or system memory) do you have in your computer?*
Software differs in the amount of free system memory that it requires in order to operate. Unless you plan on adding more memory at the same time, don't buy software for which the RAM requirements exceed the memory now available on your computer.

- *If you have an internal hard drive, what is its capacity?* It's desirable to have an internal hard drive that can accommodate all of the software that you wish to install, with storage capacity for the files you create. An average hard drive is about forty megabytes in capacity, and the average drawing or painting software application will occupy two to six megabytes of available hard-disk space.

- *How much time and money do you have to invest?*
Some programs come with more features than others and may be time-consuming to learn as well as expensive. Sometimes, a simpler, less expensive program will serve the novice's needs perfectly.

TYPES OF SOFTWARE: 'DRAW' V 'PAINT' PROGRAMS

Draw programs create shapes by mathematically generating vectors (or points and curves). By moving and clicking a mouse, the user manipulates different tools to create shapes on-screen. These shapes can then be rotated, scaled, copied and revised. Like paper cut-outs, the shapes can be arranged in layers while you work on the design; moving or overlaying shapes will not alter the shapes themselves or what is behind them. The software can continually update the position of all items in the drawing.

Some software will also allow you to use scans of sketches as drawing templates. If, for example, you wanted to create a design based on a photo or drawing,

---

Macintosh is a registered trademark of Apple Computer, Inc.

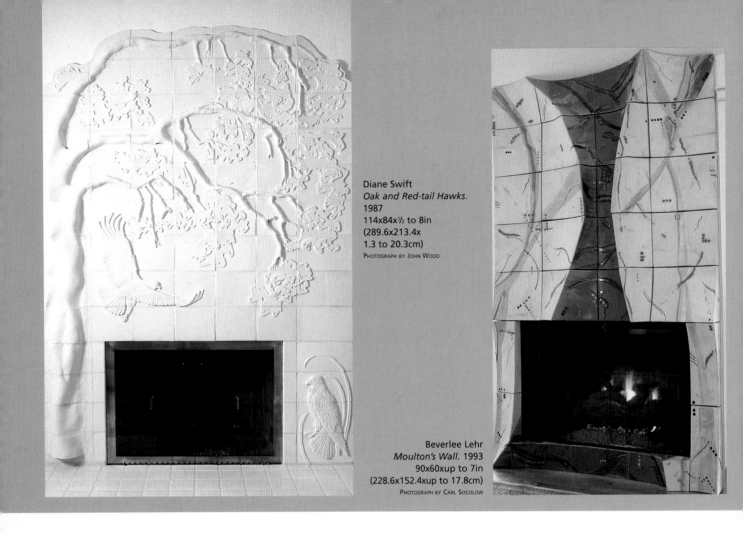

Diane Swift
Oak and Red-tail Hawks.
1987
114x84x½ to 8in
(289.6x213.4x
1.3 to 20.3cm)
PHOTOGRAPH BY JOHN WOOD

Beverlee Lehr
Moulton's Wall. 1993
90x60xup to 7in
(228.6x152.4xup to 17.8cm)
PHOTOGRAPH BY CARL SOCOLOW

you would first have a scan made up for you at a commercial bureau or make one yourself at a computer rental centre – unless, of course, you own a scanner. Next, you would take the floppy disk containing the scan to your home computer. In the drawing program, you can open a template – a greyed version of your scan. This will function as a guide that you can use while you draw on-screen; the process is similar to drawing on a piece of tracing paper. (Note that the template will not print.) You'll even find programs that offer automatic template tracing.

Draw programs are well suited to tile design because designs with repeating elements can be made and revised easily and quickly and because prints from these programs (which you'll need in order to transfer your design), are smooth edged when printed from a laser printer, due to their mathematical description.

One disadvantage to draw programs, however, is that they take longer to master; the process of drawing with a mouse can be tricky. Another is that some draw programs don't work in the 'preview' mode. If you wished to create a design with solid elements (outlined star shapes filled with colour, for example), you would draw the outlines of those shapes and could only view them as outlines while actively drawing. You must stop drawing and preview the drawing to see its solid areas of colour and different line weights. You can switch views as often as you like, but you can't draw and preview simultaneously unless you have two windows open at the same time.

Paint programs create shapes on a grid of *pixels* (or squares) that make up the page on your screen, much as coloured tiles make up a mosaic. Programs that use the grids are also called *bitmap* programs. With a mouse, the user changes the colours of the squares in order to form shapes by drawing on-screen with a tool. You can start from scratch, or a pencil sketch can be scanned, opened with the paint software, and further developed with the program's painting and editing tools. Most paint programs also have copy, scale and rotate commands of *selections* (groups of pixels). This can sometimes create problems, however, because to move the squares of a bitmap, you must literally pick up the pixels and displace them, leaving behind a hole. When you place the selection of pixels on top of another area, the pixels underneath are then erased. If you wish to enlarge a selection, a jagged appearance on the edges of the shape results, as if it were built of large squares instead of additional smaller squares. This is called *loss of resolution*. Resolution is also very important in printing from a paint program; low-resolution documents print poorly, with jagged lines and edges, while high-resolution files print better but tend to be large and to take a sizeable amont of hard-disk storage.

The advantage of paint programs is that their more direct method of operation is a little easier to master than that of draw programs. Their large disadvantage for tile design, however, is that once the designs are painted, they aren't as easy to revise or edit as are those created with draw programs.

Katy Cauker
Twist & Shout. 1988
54x30x½in
(137.2x76.2x1.3cm)
PHOTOGRAPH BY KATH LEEN

Susan Beere (from design by Erik Voght)
Banana Leaf Mural. 1989
48x96in (121.9x243.8cm)
PHOTOGRAPH BY HUGH L. WILKERSON

Susan Beere
Egret's View. 1991
36x24in (91.4x61cm)
PHOTOGRAPH BY HUGH L. WILKERSON

Some software combines tools from drawing and painting programs into a single package, making it possible to experiment with elements from each.

To transfer a printed design to a plaster block for carving, use the nail-polish remover technique described on pages 52–53 but don't bother to get a photocopy. Your computer-printed design will work just as well.

The illustrations below demonstrate just a few of the ways in which design software can be used for tile designing. These designs were created with a top-quality draw program.

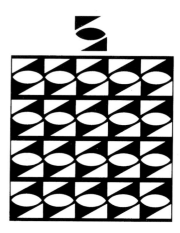

Illustration 1. Tile design based on repetitions of a single design element.

Illustration 3. Tile design consisting of two repeated design elements. Note that only segments of these elements appear around the edges of the tile.

Illustration 2. Tile design based on design element shown in Illustration 1.

Illustration 4. The same tile pattern as shown in Illustration 3, printed in reverse.

CHAPTER THIRTEEN

INSTALLATION

Fired Earth Tiles
Terracotta Stones. Ongoing
Each 3^{15}/$_{16}$x3^{15}/$_{16}$x^3/$_4$in (10x10x2cm)

Linda Dixon and Drew Krouse
Lion Fountain and Mosaic Pool. 1993
180x84x60in
(457.2x213.4x152.4cm)
PHOTOGRAPH BY LDDK STUDIOS

WHETHER OR NOT TO TRY IT

Now that you've made your tiles, what do you do with them? Designs that stand alone may be mounted just as pictures are. For instructions on making hangers, see chapter 14. Tiles, however, are really made to be installed on a permanent surface; only then do they fulfil their function as durable, decorative, hygienic surface coverings. When you see your tiles mounted and grouted as an intrinsic part of an architectural environment, you will really appreciate their worth.

Good installation can make mediocre tiles look great, and poor installation will make great tiles look mediocre, so don't skimp on installation costs. For a professional-looking job, hire a professional tiler, one who has had experience with handmade tiles, which may be thicker, heavier and more irregular than commercial tiles. Tiling is an art in itself, one that has developed over generations; you're not likely to learn this highly specialized skill overnight.

If you're a skilled craftsperson who is competent with tools and experienced in construction techniques, you're certainly capable of learning how to install your own tiles, but you'll need to practise in order to become proficient. Working with an experienced tiler will teach you many 'tricks of the trade' that will make installation work proceed more easily and efficiently. Unless you are already versed in tile installation techniques, start with a relatively simple project such as the one covered in this chapter – a small tabletop.

ADHESIVES

Always use the correct type of adhesive material for the surface that you intend to cover.

- *Thinset adhesive (or mastic)* comes in 1 quart to 5 gallon (1.1 litre to 21.1 litre) containers and is used on drywall or on thoroughly cured concrete walls. It's not made for use on floors or plywood. Tiles installed with thinset must be completely dry and should be dry-cut with a tile cutter.

- *Multi-purpose adhesive* can be used on drywall, cured concrete, or plywood, and is used for wall, floor, counter and tabletop installations. The tiles and the mounting surface must be dry and dust free. The pre-mixed adhesive comes in amounts ranging from 1 quart to 5 gallons (1.1 litre to 21.1 litres) and is the best choice for a small project like a plywood tabletop.

- *Thinset cement*, which is mixed with water, is usually used on damp or wet concrete slabs, walls or floors. The mounting surface, which is first wiped with a damp sponge to remove all dust, need not dry before the adhesive is installed. Because thinset cement will adhere to wet tiles, it is ideal for use on tiles cut with a wet saw. It comes in 50lb (22.8kg) bags and is mixed with water to a creamy consistency.

- *Thinset cement with a bonding agent* is just what it sounds like. The bonding agent is a milky-looking

Gloria Kosco
Fireplace, #2, 1989.
58x63x15in
(147.3x160x40.6cm)
PHOTOGRAPH BY JOHN HOENSTINE

liquid that is mixed with thinset cement in a ratio of 2gal (8.5 litres) bonding agent to 50lb (22.8kg) thinset. The bonding agent gives elasticity to the mixture so that it will adhere to surfaces other than concrete – to plywood, for example. The mixture is very strong and can be used on either walls or floors.

• *Epoxy thinset* consists of three ingredients that must be mixed together: one-third Part A liquid epoxy, one-third Part B liquid epoxy, and one-third powdered filler. Epoxy thinset comes in quart (1.1 litre) and gallon (4.2 litre) packages and can be used on most dry surfaces. Because it's significantly more expensive than other adhesives, it's most often used for setting irregular tiles on metal. At one time, epoxy thinset was the strongest adhesive available, but thinsets with bonding agents are now just as strong.

• The term *mud set* refers to a traditional installation method in which tiles are set directly into *mud* (or wet cement). This is a craft with ancient origins, one that should only be attempted by a professional tiler who is experienced in it. When executed correctly, mud setting is the most permanent installation method, as evidenced by ancient tile work that is still intact at historical sites such as Pompeii and Rome. Mud job techniques are too involved for inclusion here, but detailed information on mud setting is available.

• *Grout* is a form of cement that is used to fill and seal the joints between installed tiles. Grouts come in various colours; white grout is traditionally used for walls, and a natural grey colour, which won't show dirt, is often used on floors.

Some grouts also contain sand. These are used for floor tiles, handmade tiles, and for any tile installation with wide grout lines. For high-gloss tiles and tile installations with narrow grout lines, use a grout without sand.

TOOLS
Every installation project has an element that's unique; your materials, tools, and techniques should be chosen accordingly.

• *Buttering trowels* are sturdy, spatula-like tools, which come in various sizes and shapes and which are usually made with pointed or squared-off blades. They are used to apply adhesive to the backs of tiles (a process known as *buttering*) or to transfer adhesive from a bucket to the mounting surface.

• *Toothed trowels*, used to spread the adhesive over the mounting surface, are usually rectangular and have toothed edges of various sizes and shapes (Photo 68). As the trowel is used, its teeth create spaces between the raised beads of applied adhesive that are shaped by the tool's notches. Then, when the tile is pressed into the adhesive bed, the adhesive spreads into these spaces. A ¹/₂in (1.3cm) toothed trowel, therefore, will give a ¹/₄in (.6cm) adhesive bed once the tile is in place, and a ¹/₄in (.6cm) trowel will give an ¹/₈in (.3cm) bed. In general, the bigger and heavier the tiles, the larger the notches should be between the teeth of the trowel you select.

For handmade tiles, use a ¹/₄in to ¹/₂in (.6cm to 1.3cm) toothed trowel. If the back of the tile isn't completely flat, you may need to use a buttering tool to apply adhesive to the tile as well as to the mounting surface.

• *Rubber floats* are trowel-like tools with thick, soft rubber surfaces. They're used for spreading grout over and between the tiles.

• *Large sponges* and *buckets of water* should be kept on hand. You'll be cleaning surfaces and tools continually as you work.

• *Tile nips* are plier-like tools, the jaws of which have sharp, flat teeth. They're used to nip off small pieces from commercial tiles when you make a mosaic or to cut tiles to fit around obstructions such as pipes. Always wear safety glasses and heavy gloves when you use these tools.

With thick handmade tiles, tile nips are less reliable and may crack the tile. A wet saw, a hand-held, diamond-tipped, rotary blade, or a jigsaw with a carbon blade may do a better job.

• *Tile cutters* have blades that snap straight cuts across thin, flat tiles. These tools may not work on handmade relief tiles, which are often too large, thick or irregular for cutters to handle; it's best to use a wet saw instead.

• A *wet saw* is a tool for professionals; it's large and it can be expensive. In addition to cutting throughtiles of almost any size or shape, a wet saw can easily cut bevelled edges on the thickest of handmade tiles. When the tool is in use, its diamond-carbide blade is continuously lubricated with water.

• *Protective gloves* and a *mask* should always be worn when you work with chemical adhesives, cements and grouts. If you work without gloves, your skin may dry out and crack, especially around the fingertips. Use a good hand lotion even if you do wear gloves. An approved dust and mist mask is also a must whenever you work with cement; the cement-mixing process creates clouds of dust.

• *Cleaning materials* should be kept handy. Make sure that you have plenty of sponges, buckets of water and towels. Clean all your tools with water as soon as

Opposite page, left:
Frank Giorgini
Ribbed System. 1993
Each 6x6in (15.2x15.2cm)
<small>PHOTOGRAPH BY BOBBY HANSSON</small>

Opposite page, right:
Susan E. Kowalczyk
Untitled; earthenware floor detail.
1985
120x120in (304.8x304.8cm)
<small>PHOTOGRAPH BY DAVID H. RAMSEY</small>

Above: Shel Neymark
Deco Sideboard Table and Lamp.
1989
Table: 30x14x60in
(76.2x35.6x152.4cm)
Lamp: 28in (71.1cm) high.
<small>PHOTOGRAPH BY MARK KANE</small>

Right: Peter King and Marni Jaime
Mizneresque. 1992
70x74in (177.8x188cm)
<small>PHOTOGRAPH BY GARY LANGHAMMER</small>

Above: Mathers Rowley
Caribbean Coral Reef Scene (detail). 1992
Overall: 84x276in (213.4x701cm)

Left: Peter Sohngen
Building Blocks (detail). 1991
29x37in (73.7x94cm)

Opposite page: Elyse Saperstein
Legends (detail). 1990
32x120x2in (81.3x304.8x5.1cm)
PHOTOGRAPH BY JOHN CARLANO

you've finished with them, or the installation materials will harden, and removal will be nearly impossible. Most of the materials are water soluble and will be easy to remove if you act quickly.

INSTALLATION ON A TABLETOP

The instructions that follow can be applied to installing handmade tiles on almost any horizontal surface.

Before you cut your plywood tabletop to size, it's important to create a layout and to estimate the width of the grout lines. Traditionally, tiles are set with a grout joint between them that is the thickness of a trowel blade – 1/16in (.16cm). Most handmade tiles, however, are irregular in size, so the grout lines must be wider.

To determine the width of these joints, first arrange at least 1 sq. ft (929 sq. cm) of tiles next to each other, using a framing square to square them off. If this square shape is 1/8in (.3cm) off square, you'll need a 1/4in-wide (.6cm) grout joint. If the shape is 1/4in (.6cm) off square, you'll need a 1/2in (1.3cm) grout joint. This method will ensure that the irregular edges of the tiles will fall within straight grout joints.

Next, determine the layout of your tiles, allowing for the width of the grout lines between them, by arranging them on a piece of 3/4in-thick (1.9cm) plywood. (For very complex designs made up of irregularly shaped tiles, it would be wise to lay out the entire design before starting.) As you do this, consider the edges of the table-top. One way to create an edge for your table is to attach strips of 3/4in-thick (1.9cm) plywood around the bottom edges of the tabletop; these will provide a base against which you can glue and nail strips of corner moulding (see Illustration 1). To trim your tabletop's edges with narrow tiles, place the uppermost tiles on the plywood's upper surface so that they overlap the

plywood's outer edges by the width of the narrow edges of the tiles that will adhere vertically to the table's edge (see Illustration 2). This arrangement will strengthen the edges.

Illustration 1   WOOD TRIM

Illustration 2   TILE TRIM

Once your layout is complete and allows for all tiles and grout lines, cut the 3/4in-thick (1.9cm) plywood to the desired size of the tabletop. Use carpenter's glue and screws to attach four strips of 3/4in-thick (1.9cm) plywood, 2in to 3in (5.1cm to 7.6cm) in width to the bottom surface, as shown in Illustration 3.

Before installing your tiles, make sure that the back of each one and the tabletop itself are free of dust and completely dry.

TILE LAYOUT
3/4in PLYWOOD
GLUE
3/4in PLYWOOD REINFORCING STRIP
NO. 8x1 1/4in DRYWALL SCREW

Illustration 3

Then apply an ¹/₈in- to ¹/₄in-thick (.3cm to .6cm) – depending on the thickness of the tile – layer of multi-purpose ceramic adhesive to the surface of the table (and to its edges if you'll be placing tiles on them). Press the tiles down onto the plywood. Note in Photos 69 and 70 that rather than spreading adhesive over the entire tabletop and risk having it dry out as he works, the tiler is setting the edge sections first. If your

tiles are warped, you'll need to butter (apply adhesive to) the back of each tile as well as to the mounting surface.

If your tiles differ in thickness, install the thickest tiles first and then build the adhesive up behind the thinner tiles so that their top surfaces are level with those of the thicker tiles. If your tiles are all the same thickness, you need only apply adhesive to the plywood, using a toothed

amount onto the tabletop (Photo 76). With a rubber float or a rubber squeegee held at a 45° angle, spread the grout over the tiles, pressing it into the joints (Photos 77 and 78).

trowel held at a 45° angle and spreading only as much as can be covered with tiles within twenty minutes (Photos 72 and 73). Press the tiles down into the adhesive (Photo 74) until the tabletop is covered.

If you accidentally get adhesive on a tile's surface, just use a sponge dampened with hot water to wipe it off lightly (Photo 75). Be careful not to get any water into the grout joints as you do this. After all the tiles are installed, allow twenty-four hours for the adhesive to dry.

Mix your grout with water (or, for greater strength, a grout-bonding agent) in a clean bucket until the mixture is the consistency of whipped cream. Then pour the required

76

(Photo 79). Continue to clean the table, removing the grout from your sponge by rinsing it in a bucket of water (Photo 80).

When the surface is clean, allow twenty-four hours for the grout to dry. Then buff the tabletop with a dry rag to remove the film of grout on it (Photo 81).

During this entire process, remember to clean your tools while the adhesive or grout on them is still damp.

To remove excess grout from the tiles' upper surfaces, scrape across the tiles with a rubber float or squeegee, moving the tool at a diagonal to the grout joints.

Allow the grout to set for approximately fifteen minutes and then wash the surface of the table with a damp sponge and water, smoothing out the grout joints as you do

79

77

80

78

81

CHAPTER FOURTEEN

MAKING YOUR OWN
TOOLS AND EQUIPMENT

Carrie Anne Parks
Peaches. 1991
29x23¹/₂x6in
(73.7x59.7x15.2cm)

Ellie Hudovernik
Snowshoe Rabbit with Carolling Geese. 1st Annual Christmas Tile. 1993
4³/₄x4³/₄in (12.1x12.1cm)
Photograph by Robert Hudovernik

Frank Giorgini
Afro Tile. 1986
14x14in (35.6x35.6cm)
Photograph by Bobby Hansson

Due to the large number of dimensions given in this chapter, metric conversions are not provided. For readers who are more comfortable with the metric system, conversion charts are provided on page 143.

82

MATERIALS

Making things that will help you with your tile work is easy, fun and a great way to recycle those odds and ends around the house that might otherwise end up at your local rubbish tip. Though you'll need to purchase materials to make some of the tools described in this chapter, many of the others can be made from common household items. A few wire coat-hangers, tin cans, and plastic jugs will yield more than you might think. With the help of the instructions that follow, you can transform them all into handy workshop items.

CUTTING WIRE

To make a cutting wire (shown in the upper left-hand corner of Photo 82), just thread a 20in length of wire or monofilament fishing line through holes drilled in two objects that will serve as grips – short lengths of dowel will work well. Guitar strings make good substitutes for fishing line or wire.

TEMPLATES

Templates – cut to the size and shape of your tiles – can be cut from thin plywood, Masonite, or cardboard. To use a template, just place it on your clay slab and scribe or cut around it with your potter's needle. Don't forget to calculate shrinkage before cutting your templates to size.

STORAGE CONTAINERS

Recycled glass and plastic containers with lids make fine storage containers for mixed stains, glazes and powders. The top portions of some plastic bottles make excellent funnels, too; just cut them off and invert them. Use the lower sections of the bottles as water containers.

SCULPTING, INCISING AND SCRAPING TOOLS

Photo 82 shows a number of these easy-to-make tools.

• Chopsticks make excellent sculpting tools. The bamboo from which they're made is durable, and clay won't stick to it either. Chopsticks are usually free for the asking. Whittle the ends into a variety of useful shapes (Illustration 1) and finish them off with fine sandpaper. If you have access to an electric grinder or sander, you can turn out several in no time at all. To use these tools, push and shape the clay with their ends.

• *Metal strapping* – the strong, steel banding material that is used to wrap heavy materials such as lumber and large crates – makes wonderful incising tools.

Cairo Cocalis
Birds' Feet. 1992
Each 4x4in (10.2x10.2cm)
Photograph by Elizabeth Vanderkooy

Illustration 1

Illustration 2

sharpen one end of each length to knife-blade sharpness. Then, with a pair of needle-nose pliers, carefully bend the sharpened ends into different shapes (Illustration 2). Do this slowly, as the metal is brittle and may snap. Wrap some tape around the other end, and you'll have a very efficient tool for carving fine grooved lines into your leatherhard tiles. This tool is perfect for use in the incising and inlay techniques.

•Scraping tools can be made from all sorts of scrap metal, including tin cans (Illustration 3). With metal shears, cut an oval rib shape from the side of a can; wear gloves while you do this. Flatten out the shape with a hammer and then file, sand or grind the edges smooth.

Illustration 3

Many commercial shippers have switched to strong plastic straps, but you can still locate steel strapping if you ask around.

Wear thick gloves and goggles when you fabricate these metal tools; flat metal is very sharp. Cut several 6in to 8in lengths of strapping. Using a file or grinder,

•Scrapers can also be cut from plastic containers. A heavy pair of scissors will cut through most thinner, pliable plastics, but you may need a saw to cut plastic that's thicker and more rigid. Avoid using sharp knives for this job; it's all too easy to slip and cut yourself with one. Sand the edges of these cut shapes as well.

• To make a special tool for scraping beads of glaze from the edges of a tile (Illustration 4), use either a piece of metal strapping or a piece of tin can. Just cut a 90° notch in the strapping or tin. When you run this tool along the bottom edge of the tile, the notch will remove the glaze evenly.

Illustration 4

• Hacksaw blades can be shaped into excellent scraping and sculpting tools. These blades, which are used to cut metal, are usually about 12in long and ½in wide and have very fine teeth. First, be sure that you're wearing some form of eye protection and gloves. Then take a pair of pliers and snap off a 2in length of blade; you shouldn't have any trouble breaking this brittle

metal. Use your new tool to scrape and smooth convex surfaces. To shape contours on moist or leatherhard clay, first scrape at a 45° angle to the curve and then scrape at the opposite 45° angle, so that the two scraping angles are perpendicular to each other. Alternating directions in this manner will produce a beautiful contoured surface.

This tool is also very useful for scraping smooth, recessed flat surfaces on your tiles. The rough surfaces left by its teeth can be smoothed.

• Dental tools are very helpful when you're completing detailed work. Ask your dentist if he or she has any tools that have one broken end; these rejects, no longer useful to the dentist, may be yours for the asking.

• If you have access to a grinder, even the tips of 3in-long nails can be easily ground into useful shapes.

TILE DIPPER

With one coat-hanger and a pair of pliers or metal snips, you can fabricate a tool that's perfect for dipping your tile into glaze. To make this long, V-shaped dipping tool, first cut and remove the hook from a heavy-gauge wire hanger. Straighten out both arms of the V and cut them to equal lengths. Then bend up about ½in of wire at the end of each arm to create a 90° (or greater) angle.

For larger tiles, use a whole hanger to make a longer dipper. If the tile is too big and heavy to be held in the tool just described, use a length of 1x2 or a strip of ½in-thick plywood with a couple of screws, nails, or dowels at the bottom to support the bottom edge of the tile.

HANGING DEVICES FOR TILES

An excellent device for hanging and displaying individual tiles can be made from coat-hanger wire; thicker-gauged wire will work best for heavier tiles. Cut the hooks off three wire hangers and straighten each remaining length. Then cut the straightened lengths to size and bend them as

BACK VIEW

UPPER GRIP

CENTRE SUPPORT

½in FOAM STRIP

LOWER GRIP

Illustration 5

Another way to display an individual tile is to mount it on a piece of plywood, as shown below. Cut a piece of ½in-thick plywood, about ½in to 1½in smaller than your tile. Using a hole saw in an electric drill, cut a ½in to 2in diameter hole in the upper middle area of the wood. Drill two holes into the bottom edge of the plywood, about 1in from each side. Place two 'L' hooks in these holes to support the bottom edge of the tile. To gauge the hook depth correctly, carefully centre the plywood on the back of your tile. Then turn the 'L' hooks into their holes until the touch the tile's bottom edge. For a more finished appearance, spray-paint the edges of the wood.

SIDE VIEW

BRAD

½in PLYWOOD

2in DIA. HOLE

WALL

FELT PAD

'L' HOOK

Illustration 6

shown in Illustration 5, in proportion to the tile for which you're making the hanger. If the hanger fits your tile too loosely, bend its top and bottom arms back on themselves to add some tension.

A strip of ½in foam wedged between the lower back of the tile and the wire support will ensure that the tile hangs parallel to the wall and doesn't tilt to the left or right. To protect the front surface of your tile, slip small lengths of clear plastic tubing (available at hardware or pet shops) over the hooked ends of the wire.

Fix the tile to the plywood with multi-purpose adhesive, silicone glue or any good tile adhesive, pushing the tile down so that its bottom edge rests on the hooks. These hooks will counter the force of gravity that will always pull on your tile. When the glue is dry, hang your tile by placing the hole over a nail. A few stick-on felt pads placed on the back of the wood will protect the wall. Because the tips of the two bottom hooks will be barely visible, the tile will appear to float on the wall.

MURAL HANGER

The long bevelled strips on the wall and mural-hanging device shown in Illustration 7 serve to distribute the mural's weight evenly against the mounting surface.

To construct this mounting board, first select a good grade of ³⁄₄in-thick plywood that is finished on one side. Lay your mural out on the finished side, allowing for grout spaces if applicable, and trace around its perimeter. Square off the sides and then cut the plywood to size.

Next, reinforce the panel by using countersunk wood screws of an appropriate length to attach four ³⁄₄x3in strips of plywood to the rear of the plywood mounting board. Cut two equal lengths from the same strip material and cut a 45° bevel along one long edge of each. Attach one strip to the back of the plywood, with its bevelled edge facing down, and the other to the mounting surface, with its

bevelled edge facing up. Be sure that the strip on the mounting surface is attached to the studs in the wall. To mount your completed mural, just rest one bevelled strip along the bevelled edge of the other, and gravity will hold the mural hanger in place.

To make a more attractive mural hanger, first refer to the photograph above, entitled *Chameleons in the Night*. Note that the tiles, which are set back about ½in from the aluminium frame around them, rest on plywood that has been painted black. The plywood back of this hanging device was cut 1in wider and 1in longer than the temporarily assembled mural tiles. A frame was then welded from ¼in-thick, 2in aluminium angle stock; it was just large enough to enable me to drop the plywood back right into its interior. The frame was attached to the back of the plywood with screws.

A wooden reinforcement frame was attached to the back. This was made with strips of wood that would allow the aluminium frame to set at the desired height in relation to the thickness of the mounted tiles. A thicker bevelled strip was attached to its back, to allow for the aluminium frame. I added a second strip to keep the bottom of the mural from tilting back against the wall.

TOOLS FOR CUTTING SHAPES FROM SLABS

If you're handy and have access to certain tools, it's not very difficult to make 'pastry cutter' devices (Photo 83) with which to cut tile shapes from a clay slab. Don't forget to take tile shrinkage into account as you design the tools' final shapes and dimensions. And put on a pair of thick gloves; working with metal can be dangerous.

First, cut a piece of ³⁄₄in-thick scrap wood to the shape that you'd like your tile to be. Use screws to attach a thin metal strip (the galvanized metal from which heating ducts are made works well) around the outer edges of the wooden shape and flush with its top surface. Make sure that the strip is wide enough to cut through the clay slab

HANGER

MURAL

HANGER

PLYWOOD
BACKER

PLYWOOD
FRAME

WAll

SIDE VIEW

Illustration 7

OPEN-FACE MOULD FORMS

To make a mould form for a handmade relief tile, first refer to Photo 22 on page 44. In the upper left-hand corner of this photograph is an adjustable mould form called a cottle. It is made from ³/₄x8x20in pieces of countertop material, the smooth formica sides of which face inward. (Cottles can vary in size and in the materials from which they're made.) To one end of each cottle is fastened a ³/₄x1¹/₂x8in piece of wood; scraps of the countertop board can also be used to make these blocks. Use glue and No. 6 x 1¹/₂in countersunk wood screws to secure these blocks, making sure to fasten them to the outside surfaces of the cottle pieces.

When you're ready to make a plaster mould, position two of the cottle boards on edge and fasten them with a C-clamp. Take care not to let go of the boards as you do this, or they'll fall right on top of your model. Then fasten the remaining boards with three more C-clamps, adjusting the boards so that they form an enclosed area that is large enough to allow for a 1¹/₂in to 2in space between the inner surface of each wall and the outer edge of the relief tile. Check the cottle for square and make sure that the tile model is equidistant from all four inner surfaces of the form. Then seal the bottom edges and corners of the form, as described in chapter 5.

Mould forms may also be made by cutting bevelled lengths of 2x4 to specific lengths for specific tile projects and holding them together with a web or band clamp. The forms shown on the right-hand side of Photo 22 on page 44 consist of four 13in-long (O.D.) lengths of 2x4 that have been cut to allow for a 1³/₄in space between the inner walls of the form and the edges of the tile model. Each end of each piece is bevelled at 45°. Place the lengths on edge and strap them together with a web (or band) clamp. Note that this form is not adjustable.

To calculate the dimensions of these forms, start with the dimensions of your tile model – 4¹/₂x4¹/₂in, for example. Add between 3in and 4in to each dimension – the combined distance between the edges of the tile model

83

and that all corners are bent cleanly. Because your slab is likely to be ³/₈in to ¹/₂in thick, the strip should be about 2in wide.

To make a plunger mechanism that will release your cut tiles from the cutter, first drill a couple of ¹/₂in holes through the wood shape. Then insert two 3in-long dowels, each ¹/₂in thick, through the holes. Cut a Masonite or thin plywood template that is just a bit smaller than the wood shape and position it on the bottom of the shape so that it's surrounded by the metal edging material; it should be loose enough to have some play. Attach the Masonite to the dowels with countersunk screws. To make a handle for the plunger, fasten a strip of wood to the two dowels. Many variations of this design are possible.

PLASTER-BLOCK MOULD FORMS

Following are directions for making two types of mould forms. The first is used to make a plaster mould from an original relief tile. The second is a form with which you can produce several plaster blocks at a time for carving and pressing out relief tiles. (See chapters 5 and 6 for descriptions of these pressing techniques.)

and two opposing sides of the form. This figure (8in, for example) will give you the inner dimensions of the form. Cut a 45° end on your 2x4, measure and mark the calculated length on its short face, flip the 2x4 over, and cut another 45° angle at the mark you made to give you a cottle wall of the correct length for your tile model. Repeat these steps to make the other three walls.

MOULD FORMS FOR MAKING MULTIPLE PLASTER BLOCKS

In order to carve plaster moulds for relief tiles (see chapter 6), you'll need solid plaster blocks. Following are instructions for a time-saving form with which you can make several of these blocks at one time. The form consists of two notched lengths of formica-coated wood, plastic or plexiglass that are held together with threaded rods and spacer strips that form multiple sections once they're placed between the notched lengths (Illustration 8). The form can also be made with plywood that has been well coated with polyurethane or clear wood sealer.

Shown in the foreground of Photo 22 on page 44 is a form that I made from 1/4in-thick scrap plexiglass. When cutting plexiglass, protect yourself against airborne shards by wearing protective clothing, gloves and goggles. Formica is a safer alternative, and the plaster will release from it very well because formica is so smooth. When kitchen countertops are made, the kitchen sink cut-outs

are often discarded. Try to find a couple of these scraps at a furniture shop.

Before constructing this form, you will need to calculate shrinkage for the tiles that you'll be making with your plaster blocks; once you've made this calculation, you can determine the correct size of each square in the form.

The cross pieces can be made from any one of several materials. To make them from formica, glue the backs of two formica strips together so that their smooth sides are facing out. Masonite or lattice can also be used; just be sure to coat wood surfaces with polyurethane. Sheets of 1/8in-thick plastic are also available at hardware shops. These make excellent cross pieces because their width is the same as the width of most crosscut saw blades; making a notch for one in the side piece is as easy as making a single pass with the blade. The sheets are cut with a craft-knife blade designed for cutting plastic.

Cut two side pieces, each about 2ft long and 2in wide. Then cut notched grooves, about 3/16in deep and as wide as the cross pieces that will be fitted into them, making sure to cut these on the smooth face of each side piece. The dimensions between the notches on each side piece should equal the width of your plaster block. When you cut the cross pieces to size, remember to add the depth of your notches on each side to their length, or two sides of your plaster block will be shorter than you'd like.

Then centre and drill 1/4in holes through each side piece,

NOTCHED SIDE BOARD

CROSS PIECE

GLASS BOTTOM

WASHER

WING NUT

1/4in THREADED ROD

MOIST CLAY

GLASS

Illustration 8

Laird Plumleigh
Octopus. 1990
22¹/₂x22¹/₂x4in (57.2x57.2x10.2cm)
PHOTOGRAPH BY PHILLIP RITTERMAN

³/₄in from each end. Place the pieces on edge, lining them up so that the notched surfaces face each other.

Cut two lengths of ¹/₄in threaded rod to fit through the holes drilled in the side pieces; these should be long enough to accommodate a washer and wing nut on each end. Insert the rods into the drilled holes, slip the cross strips into the notches, and gently tighten the wing nuts until the strips are secure. Check to see that the corners of the form are all square. Then place the assembled form on a thick sheet of glass and use moist clay to seal the outside edges between the form and the glass as well as the outside corners.

TILE-WAXING STAND

This handy device (Illustration 9) will help you to wax the lower edges of your tiles in preparation for dipping the tiles into the glaze. You place the tile (face up) on the foam-padded platform and then use one hand to apply the wax with a foam brush as you use the other to rotate the stand on a turntable. Next, lift the tile off the stand, hold it upside-down in one hand, and use the foam brush to wax the entire back.

When you're waxing many tiles, use the stand to support the tile during the first stage of the waxing process to help you keep your supporting arm from getting tired. Keep the tile flat and face up to prevent the wax from running across the surface that you want to glaze; gravity carries the wax down towards the bottom of the tile instead.

To build this simple stand, first rip an approximately 24in-long piece of 1³/₄x3¹/₂in pine into two 1³/₄in-wide lengths. One of these pieces will serve as the post; cut it to a length that will be comfortable for you once the completed stand is sitting on the turntable – perhaps 18in. From the other piece, cut a 10in length to serve as the brace. Then, to make the base, cut a 10x10x³/₄in piece of plywood or pine. The foam support is also cut from ³/₄in-thick wood; its width and length should be 1in smaller than the tiles on which you're working. For 3x6in tiles, for example, cut a 2x5in foam support. Finally, cut a piece of ¹/₂in-thick foam to the size of the foam support.

To assemble the waxing stand, first position the brace on

¹/₂x2 x 5in
FOAM PAD

NO. 8x3in
DRYWALL
SCREW

³/₄x2x5in
PAD SUPPORT

1³/₄x1³/₄x18in POST

1³/₄x1³/₄x10in
BRACE

NO. 8x2¹/₂in
DRYWALL
SCREW

³/₄x10x10in
BASE

NO. 8x2in
DRYWALL
SCREW

TURNTABLE

Illustration 9

the base so that one of its sides will be flush against the base of the centre post once it's attached. Fasten it in place with two No. 8 x 2in drywall screws, inserted from the bottom of the base. Then centre the post in the middle of the base with one face against the brace. Fasten the post to the brace with No. 8 x 2¹/₂in drywall screws, as shown in the illustration. Also insert one screw through the bottom of the base and into the centre post. To attach the foam support to the top of the post, centre it on the post and then insert two No. 8 x 2in drywall screws through its face. Glue the foam to the support with rubber cement.

Andrea Rudner
Star Mosaic. 1993
Image: 7x9in (17.8x22.9cm)

Opposite page, left:
Diana and Tom Watson
*Brentwood Plaza
Stair Risers.* 1993
Each 4½x4½in
(11.4x11.4cm)
PHOTOGRAPH BY DIANA WATSON

Hanna Lore Hombordy
Round Shell Tile. 1989
12in diameter (30.5cm diameter)
PHOTOGRAPH BY HANNA LORE HOMBORDY

SLAB CUTTER

Used to cut small, tile-sized slabs of clay that are uniform in thickness, this tool is my own invention and makes the process of cutting multiple slabs quite easy. Its operating principle, depicted in Photo 84, is simple. The tool is placed on a block of clay and the cutting wire is pulled across the metal edges of the tool to slice off slabs of a thickness determined by the distance between the edge of the angle irons and the bottom surface of the Masonite pad attached to the underside of the base. For specific instructions on how to use the slab cutter, see page 48.

On this particular model, constructed from scrap material, I used 8in-long, 90° angle irons to create the metal edges across which the wire is pulled. As an alternative to the angle irons, I could have attached ¼in-thick lattice strips or thin metal strips to the two edges of the 6x8in base. By doing this, I could easily change the thickness of my slabs whenever I wanted to, just by exchanging those strips for others of a different width. For my purposes, however – the production of six hundred identical tiles – the angle irons worked well.

To make sure that each slab was cut to a particular thickness, I attached a piece of Masonite (slightly longer and wider than the slabs I wanted to cut) to the underside of the base. (The pad is visible in Illustration 10 but not in Photo 84.) The ⅞in width of an angle iron's arm minus the ⅛in thickness of the pad equalled the ¾in thickness of my desired slab.

Apart from the dimensions that determine the thickness of the slabs to be cut, the dimensions of the other parts of this tool may vary quite a bit. The handle does need to be long enough to allow the wire to be cut across the entire block of clay. I used a 24in long 1x3 furring strip. The base is 6x8in, but these dimensions may be smaller or larger depending upon the desired size of the slabs.

HANDLE

1x6x8in TOP

WIRE

1 x 8in ANGLE

WIRE GRIP

MASONITE
SPACER

TOP VIEW   BOTTOM VIEW

CLAY IN BAG

Illustration 10

Dale Wiley
Scarab. 1987
5x5¾in (12.7x14.6cm)
PHOTOGRAPH BY PETER VON WILKEB ZOOK

84

If you use lattice strips rather than angle irons, you can avoid splitting the lattice as you attach it to the edges of the base by pre-drilling holes in it before inserting the ¾in wood screws. If you do use angle irons, attach them to the base with ½in-long screws.

Though the dimensions of your slab cutter's parts may vary, the assembly procedure is fairly straightforward. Attach the angle irons, lattice strips or metal strips to the base first. If you use the angle irons, centre and glue the Masonite pad to the underside of the base, making sure that its smooth surface faces outwards.

One end of the handle may be bevelled at 45°, as shown in Photo 84, but this step isn't necessary. Mark locations for the five screws that will fasten the handle to the base. Then, centred about 1½in from the opposite end of the handle, drill a ¼in hole through the handle's face. Measure and mark a point centred 3½in from the same end and insert a small screw eye at that point, with the eye in the handle's bottom surface.

Fasten the handle to the base with five countersunk No. 6 x 1¼in wood screws. Then fasten one end of the wire to the screw eye. Monofilament line makes a good

substitute; though it will wear out more quickly, it won't fray as braided wire will. Cut the wire's other end so that about 12in of wire extends beyond the base. To make a grip for the wire, wrap this loose end around a short length of dowel. Loop some wire or string through the hole in the handle's end so that you can hang up the slab cutter when it's not in use.

GIORGINI STUDIO TILE PRESS

The tile press featured in Photos 85 and 86 is my original design. It's used to press out tiles from either carved-block or open-face moulds. For instructions on how to use it, refer to chapter 6.

The design is based on that of traditional manual presses used by tile manufacturers around the turn of the 20th century. Pressure applied by means of a simple lever-and-plunger mechanism serves to press moist clay into (or onto) a plaster mould.

Expensive hydraulic studio presses with air-pressure release moulds are available, as are plans for making one yourself, but they're more complex to build than mine, and each air-release mould that you make for one of

85

Opposite page: Jerry Wellman
Portraits (detail). 1993
Each 4¼x4¼in
(10.8x10.8cm)

Frank Giorgini
Sea Life. 1985
Mounted mural: 28x42in (71.1x106.7cm)
PHOTOGRAPH BY JOHN LAWRENCE

these presses takes a considerable investment. For greater production capability, however, they are useful.

This design can be made from standard timber and plywood and from pipe fittings that are available from any hardware or plumbing supplier. Only simple hand tools and readily available hardware are required. The lightweight press, which will outperform most commercially available hand presses, is also compact; it takes up only 2ft of counter space. And it's durable, too. In fact, the original model has been in service at Parsons School of Design, in New York City, for eight years and has not required any maintenance or repair.

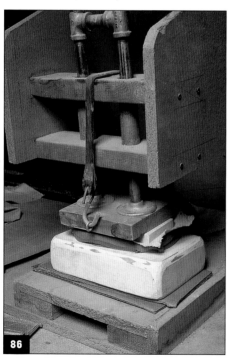

SUGGESTED TOOLS

Circular saw
Jigsaw or saber saw
³⁄₈in Variable-speed drill
⁷⁄₆₄in Drill bit
1¼in Spade bit
Countersink bit
No. 2 Phillips screwdriver
No. 2 Phillips power-drive bit
³⁄₁₆in Straight-bladed screwdriver
Hammer
Round wood rasp
Tape measure
24in Straight-edge
Pipe wrenches
Sandpaper
Safety goggles

REQUIRED TIMBER

| 1 | ³⁄₄in x4ftx4ft | C-D Plywood or chipboard |
| 1 | 1½x3½inx8ft | Yellow pine or Douglas fir (Stress-graded 2x4s) |

PLUMBING FITTINGS

1	1inx5ft	Galvanized pipe (threaded one end)
1	1x³⁄₄in	Galvanized reducer coupling
1	³⁄₄x2in	Galvanized nipple
1	³⁄₄in	Galvanized Tee
1	½x11½in	Galvanized pipe (threaded both ends)
4	½in	Galvanized pipe floor flanges
2	½x16in	Galvanized pipe (threaded both ends)
2	½in	Galvanized elbows
1	½x2in	Galvanized nipple
2	1x6in	Heavy-wall black boiler pipe (Schedule 80 XS) Note: When you have these two cut, request that the inside burrs on the cut ends not be reamed out.
1	1¼x30in	Galvanized pipe (optional)

HARDWARE AND SUPPLIES

4	No. 20	Worm-drive hose clamps (1⁵/₁₆in diameter)
2	No. 12	Worm-drive hose clamps (¹³/₁₆in diameter)
3	No. 8 x 1⁹/₁₆in	Screw eyes
16	No. 10 x ³/₄in	Flathead wood screws
48	No. 8 x 2in	Drywall screws
8	No. 8 x 1¹/₄in	Drywall screws
1	12in	Flat rubber tie-down strap
1	15in	Flat rubber tie-down strap

CONSTRUCTION PROCEDURE

1. Transfer the layout provided in Illustration 11 onto the 4x4ft sheet of plywood or chipboard. Double-check your measurements before cutting because the pieces are arranged on the board in a specific pattern. Don't worry about the rounded corners just yet; they'll be marked and cut in Step 4.

2. Put on your safety goggles and use a circular saw to cut out the nine pieces. Cut the single 48in centreline first in order to split the panel. Then cut the diagonal, followed by the two 24in cuts and the three 12in cuts. (The only two scrap pieces – the 5x6in pieces shown in the upper right-hand corner of Illustration 11 -- can be saved to place under your canvas, clay and block when you're using the tile press.)

3. From the 8ft 2x4, cut two 24in lengths and two 12in lengths. (You'll use the leftover piece to brace the lever out of harm's way; see Step 18.)

4. Lay out and trim the two side pieces, as shown in Illustration 12. (Save the 9x12in cut-outs. One will be used to make the shimmed pad described in Step 15; the other can be used to make pounding blocks for relief tiles.) Shape the rounded corners by tracing around the bottom of a 13oz (369ml) coffee jar; their radii are about 2in. Note that the upper front edge of the press is first cut back by 1¹/₄in. On both sides of each side piece, mark the placement of the two 12in front cross supports; these positions are determined from the cut-back edge. The pipe-flange

Illustration 11

Illustration 12

George F. Fishman
Jubilee. 1989
32x48in (81.3x121.9cm)

pivots at the rear are centred 2³/₄in from the rear and upper edges of the press; mark these positions on the inside face of each piece.

5. Place the 12x24in inside bottom section on top of the two 24in 2x4s so that the long edges are flush on both sides (see Illustration 13). Drill a series of ⁷/₆₄in holes down each side, 5in apart and 2in in from the edges. Use the countersink bit to recess the hole openings. Then fasten the assembly with ten No. 8 x 2in drywall screws, using the power-drive bit in your drill.

6. Centre this completed assembly on the 24x24in bottom section so that the lower board extends 6in from each side, and the front and back are flush (see Illustration 13). Mark for placement. Flip the whole thing over and draw two lines, each parallel to the 2x4s underneath and 7¹/₂in in from an edge of the bottom section. Then drill another series of ⁷/₆₄in holes, 5in apart, along these lines. Fasten the assembly to the bottom section by countersinking and fastening screws through these holes as before.

7. Fasten one of the two pipe flanges at the marked position on the inside of one side piece, using No. 10 x ³/₄in screws (see Illustration 14). Mark the position for the other flange on the other side piece. Fasten it in place with No. 10 x ³/₄in screws and then unfasten it. (Creating the screw holes in this manner will make final fastening easier.)

Illustration 14

Turn the base assembly upright and attach the side piece with the flange already on it to one edge of the inside bottom section, using seven No. 8 x 2in drywall screws along the side. Space the ⁷/₆₄in holes 3in apart and countersink the openings as before.

Illustration 13

Tamara Jaeger
In the Garden. 1992
8x8in (20.3x20.3cm)
PHOTOGRAPH BY CHAS KRIDER

Frank Giorgini
Fireplace. 1991
52x52in
(132.1x132.1cm)
PHOTOGRAPH BY TOM TEICH

8. Slip one No. 12 hose clamp onto the 11½in section of ½in pipe, followed by the ¾in Tee fitting and the other No. 12 clamp (see Illustration 15). Screw the pipe into the pipe flange that is fastened to the side piece and screw the other flange on the other end of the pipe. Then fasten the other side piece in place.

9. Position the 12x12in back section between the side pieces so that its lower edge is 7in above the base. Fasten it in the same manner as before, using three No. 8 x 2in drywall screws spaced 4in apart at each side. Check to see that the sides are perpendicular to the base. Thread the unfastened pipe flange in or out as needed to meet the side piece and then screw the flange in place.

11. Place the cross-support assembly between the side pieces at the positions previously marked. Drill two 7/64in holes through the sides and into the supports at each of the four marked joints. The holes should be 2in apart, and their faces should be countersunk. Fasten with eight No. 8 x 2in drywall screws.

12. Assemble the plunger mechanism by threading the two ½in elbows onto the ½x2in nipple (see Illustration 17). Then thread the ½x16in pipes into the free ends of the elbows. Tighten the long pipes using two pipe wrenches – they both need to be the same length. Adjust the elbows on the nipple so that the pipes slip easily through the mounted cross-support pipe sleeves. Attach the pipe flanges after the plunger is installed and adjust them so that they're level.

NO. 12
HOSE CLAMP

¾in TEE

½x11½in PIPE

1x5in PIPE

¾x2in
PIPE NIPPLE

¾x1in
COUPLING

Illustration 15

10. Drill two 1¼in holes through both 12in cross supports, positioning the holes at the centreline of each piece and centring them 3½in apart (see Illustration 16). Enlarge the holes slightly with a round wood rasp until a length of 1in (i.d.) heavy-wall pipe fits snugly inside. Slip two No. 20 hose clamps onto each length of 6in heavy-wall pipe and tap the cross supports onto the pipe ends. Position and tighten the clamps so that they're against the inside faces of the two supports. (They may have to be readjusted later.)

CROSS SUPPORT

12in

3½in

3in

7in

PLUNGER BOARD

Illustration 16

13. Fasten the two 6x7in pieces together using four No. 8 x 1¼in drywall screws at the corners. The holes should be drilled with a 7/64in bit and countersunk. Then centre the board beneath the two plunger flanges, with the 7in edge facing the front, and mark the eight flange screw holes. Remove the board, drill the mounting holes, and fasten the board to the flanges with eight No. 10 x ¾in wood screws.

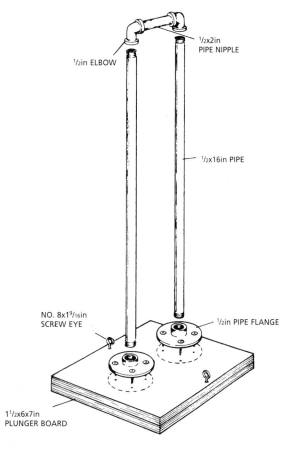

½x2in PIPE NIPPLE

½in ELBOW

½x16in PIPE

NO. 8x1⁹/₁₆in SCREW EYE

½in PIPE FLANGE

1½x6x7in PLUNGER BOARD

Illustration 17

14. Use a 7/64in bit to drill two holes in the top of the plunger board, centred near the front and rear edges. Drill a third hole, centred in the back piece of the press. Fasten a No. 8 x 1⁹/₁₆in screw eye into each of these holes. Hook the 15in rubber strap into the eye at the front of the plunger board, run it up and over the top cross support between the two plunger pipes, and pull it down to hook the eye between that rear hook and the one fastened to the back of the press (see Illustration 18).

15. Because the plunger mechanism has some free play within the pipe sleeves, the 12in strap keeps the plunger board tilted slightly forward at a consistent angle. To compensate for this minute angle, you may want to take the remaining 9x12in side cut-out and mount its front corners to the front of the inside bottom section, so that it's directly beneath the plunger board. (Use No. 8 x 1¼in screws.) Then, by shimming up the rear of that pad with flat washers or metal or wooden shims, you can make its face parallel to that of the plunger board for a perfectly

even pressing surface. Fasten the rear corners, too, once the proper angle is established.

16. To assemble the plunger lever, tighten the 1in to ¾in reducer coupling onto the 5ft length of 1in pipe (see Illustration 15). Then fasten the ¾x2in nipple onto the reducer. Tighten this entire assembly into the end of the ¾in Tee at the top of the press. Tighten the two No. 12 hose clamps at each side of the Tee fitting. The 5ft lever arm rests on top of the plunger mechanism and provides leveraged pressure. If you're strong and plan to bear down on the arm for extra pressure, slip a 30in length of 1¼in pipe over the 1in by 5ft lever arm to prevent the handle from bending.

17. Use some sandpaper and a block of wood to go over the press and remove any splintered rough edges. You can coat the whole press with polyurethane but doing so isn't necessary.

18. To protect yourself from accidental bruises, wrap the end of the lever arm with foam rubber and fasten it with attention-grabbing red tape. If possible, suspend a piece of rope with a loop in one end from the ceiling; use the loop to keep the lever arm raised and out of harm's way. Another way to keep the lever arm above eye level is to place a board (the 2x4 scrap left over from this project will work well) across the top of the press so that the lever arm rests on the board instead of the cross-supports. Fasten two screws into the top edges of the side pieces to keep the board from sliding off. When the press isn't being used, unscrew the lever arm completely and store it in a safe place.

SIDE SECTION

1x5in PIPE

½in ELBOW

½x16in ELBOW

NO. 20 HOSE CLAMP

6in SCHEDULE 80 PIPE

15in TIE DOWN

NO. 8x1⁹/₁₆in SCREW EYE

12in TIE DOWN

OPTICAL COMPENSATION BOARD

SHIM

Illustration 18

Chapter Fifteen

The Day of One Hundred Tiles

Frank Giorgini
Tile Heritage Foundation
Commemorative Tile. 1993
6x3in (15.2x7.6cm)
Photograph by Bobby Hansson

As I was writing this book, I took on a large tile assignment from the Tile Heritage Foundation (a national, non-profit organization that provides information and referrals regarding historic and contemporary tiles). This assignment was to design and produce a commemorative tile and to make six hundred replicas of it (Photo 87). I completed this task with help volunteered by friends and by students at Parsons School of Design in New York City. The finished tile is shown on the previous page.

87

As the project progressed, we learned how to improve our efficiency and production quality, and I also developed several new tools and techniques that helped to shove minutes – even hours – off production time. By the time the project was nearing completion, I was able to press out one hundred tiles, by myself, in a single day. For anyone who is considering a project of this magnitude, the technical information and time estimates that follow should prove quite valuable. Tiles as commemorative gifts, advertising handouts, awards and coasters are a very feasible outlet for your tile designs and hand-production capabilities.

I'd been asked to design a 3x6in (7.6x15.2cm) tile with 1992 and the Tile Heritage Foundation logo on it. The

design that I came up with was a 'tile on a tile', with one of my stylized lizards holding on in the background; the foreground bore the logo and date. I envisaged this tile as carved bold relief, hand-pressed, fired to medium stoneware, 2174°F (1190°C), cone 6, in electric oxidation, with a matt-green Toshika glaze that I often use, one that breaks nicely over textured surfaces and has an old look to it. This design was approved.

I rolled out a 4x8x$\frac{1}{2}$in (10.2x20.3x1.3cm) slab of moist clay and calculated shrinkage to obtain a final fired size of 3x6in (7.6x15.2cm). I cut the slab down to the model size of 3$\frac{3}{8}$x6$\frac{3}{4}$in (8.6cmx17.1cm) and drew my design roughly on it with a pin. By adding and scraping away clay, I slowly sculpted the surface into shape. I was meticulous about avoiding undercuts; I knew I had to produce many tiles from the mould, and I wanted them to release as easily and as quickly as possible.

In order to make twenty identical moulds, I first prepared the forms and poured one mould. Then I produced nineteen more tiles with this mould, and as each one came out, I immediately made another mould from it (Photo 88). The second-generation moulds had to be made right away, before the tile models had a chance to shrink significantly.

88

Opposite page, both: Lynda Curtis
Yirkalla II. 1993
Image: 16x16in
(40.6x40.6cm)
PHOTOGRAPH BY BOBBY HANSSON

Right: Randy Fein
Classical Dream. 1989
24x27x4in (61x68.6x10.2cm)

Below: Bonnie Johnson
Journey. 1986
38x38x8in (96.5x96.5x20.3cm)
PHOTOGRAPH BY STEVE duFOUR

Peter Sohngen
Hex (detail). 1989
Overall: 24x15½in
(61x39.4cm)

I kept the moulds loosely stacked in front of the fan for five days because I knew that the drier they were, the faster we could pop out the tiles.

Next, we prepared twenty 3³/₈x6³/₄x³/₄in (8.6x17.1x 1.9cm) clay plugs. At first, making these plugs was the most time-consuming step in the process. We were slicing off a slab of clay, pounding it flat with our hands, tracing a template, and then cutting each 3³/₈x6³/₄in (8.6x17.1cm) shape. To save time, we tried rolling out a large, ³/₄in-thick (1.9cm) slab on the slab roller and cutting the shapes out of that. This method proved a little quicker, but it still took more time than we wanted to spend.

This was the point at which I invented the slab cutter described on pages 48 and 122–123. By using this tool, I was able to cut twenty ³/₄in-thick (1.9cm) tile-sized slabs really quickly. I then traced a 3³/₈x6³/₈in (8.6x16.2cm) template on each slab and removed and wedged up the trimmings. The plugs were stacked with pieces of canvas between them, and the whole stack was covered with plastic. I could get twenty clay plugs from one 25lb (11.4kg) bag of clay, and after pressing the twenty tiles, we recovered about 13lb (5.9kg) of clay.

I arranged my tools and work area so that everything I needed was close at hand: a piece of cardboard on which to place the plaster mould, a soft brush, a piece of canvas, a cutting wire, a wooden straight-edge, a rubber logo stamp and, of course, the Giorgini Studio Tile Press.

The next steps had a rhythm of their own. I took a mould from the stack in front of the fan and brushed out any dry clay or dust with the brush. Then I placed the mould face up on the cardboard, took a prepared clay plug from the plastic-covered supply, and patted it down into the mould opening. I placed the canvas and a wooden block over it, positioned the mould under the plunger of the tile press, pulled down the lever, turned the mould around 180°, and pulled down the lever again. Next, I removed the mould from the press, drew the cutting wire across it, and placed the wadded-up trimmings into the plastic bag. I drew a straight-edge across the top of the mould until the back of the tile was level and pressed in the logo. Finally, I removed the mould and placed it in the stack of moulds to dry.

In less than one hour, the tiles were ready to pop out. I removed a mould from the stack, positioned it face up on the table, placed two sticks on it – one on each side of the opening – and then covered the sticks with a board. When I flipped the whole assembly over and tapped the board on the table, the tile fell right out onto the board. I lifted the mould and stacked it with the others in front of the fan. Finally, I slid the the tile off the board and onto a piece of wall-board large enough to hold twenty tiles.

Biscuit firing, glazing and glaze firing proceeded much as they're described in this book. In Chart II, you'll find suggestions as to how much time you might allow for each step of the entire process.

Chart II

Process	Allocated Time
Sculpting the model	2 weeks
Preparing 20 clay plugs	20 minutes
Pressing out 20 tiles with the studio press	40 minutes
Popping 20 tiles out of the moulds and stacking the moulds	20 minutes
Drying time (uncovered)	4 to 7 days
Loading 150 bone-dry tiles in electric kiln for biscuit firing at 1886°F (1030°C), cone 05	1 hour
Biscuit firing at 1886°F (1030°C), cone 05	13 hours
Cooling in the kiln	15 hours
Waxing the sides and back of 100 tiles	1.5 hours
Dipping 100 tiles in glaze and cleaning wax from backs and sides	3.5 hours
Loading 100 tiles into kiln for glaze firing	1.5 hours
Glaze firing at 1841°F (1005°C), cone 06	13 hours
Cooling in the kiln	15 hours
Unloading the kiln	1 hour

HEALTH AND SAFETY

Emily Goodman
Sweet Peas. Abstract, Pig and Coffee Cup. 1990
Each 5⁷⁄₈x5⁷⁄₈in (14.9x14.9cm)
PHOTOGRAPH BY DAVID F. MANSURE © 1993

Even for the novice tile maker, safety and health should be primary considerations, so read this section carefully. For more detailed information, you should refer to *Health and Safety in Ceramics*, published by the British Institute of Ceramics, which gives guidelines on the handling and use of materials and equipment, studio set-up, techniques and procedures.

The two primary concerns that you will have if you're working at home are the nature of the materials that you'll be using and the firing process. Clays, underglazes, glazes, oxides and stains may all contain health-hazardous substances. When they're fired they may also release dangerous gases, vapours and fumes.

HOME STUDIOS

The best home studio is the one that isn't a part of the home at all; it should be located in a shed or garage or in a basement that has its own entrance. This separation will help to keep air-borne dust particles, gases and fumes out of your living space.

If you must work in your home, be sure that the space you choose is kept completely closed off from the rest of the house and is used for no other purpose. Work only with clays (not glazes) in that space and avoid dusty processes such as mixing glazes, sanding green ware and reprocessing clay. (If you plan to create dust, work out of doors instead.)

If it's given a chance, clay dust will hitch a ride on your shoes, clothing or body. Don't let it. Get a set of protective work clothes (avoid flammable synthetic fabrics) and a pair of shoes; when you leave the studio, clean up and leave them behind.

CLEANLINESS

Keeping yourself and your studio clean is especially important. Wash your work clothing frequently, keeping it separate from all other clothing. After working with glazes or underglazes, wash your hands carefully, using a nail-brush when you do – and always wash before you leave the studio.

Whenever you can, work 'wet' and clean 'wet'. The less you move dust around, the better. Plan your work area with clean-up procedures in mind. Seal the floors and make sure that they're waterproof. Make or purchase tables, shelving, and equipment that can be sponged clean – and then sponge them clean when they need it. Wipe up spills right away. Clean compulsively!

TOOLS AND EQUIPMENT

Keep all your tools and equipment in good condition. Because you'll be working with water, pay particular attention to the condition of electrical tools and to the condition of your home or workshop wiring.

KILNS

Kilns can be hazardous on two fronts: fire in any form is a danger, of course, and your tiles – as well as the substances on them – can emit dangerous chemicals during the firing process. If you're a beginner, don't construct a kiln of your own. Handmade kilns are definitely not a project to undertake until you are an expert. And don't fire anything in your kiln until you've had a proper ventilation system installed.

Electric kilns should be equipped with canopy hoods and negative pressure ventilation systems or isolated in a separate room that is provided with very rapid dilution ventilation. Stacks on fuel-fired kilns should be tall enough to keep emissions from floating into areas where they're not wanted. Unless these kilns are located out of doors, they should also be equipped with canopy hoods to collect emissions and gases during firing techniques such as reduction firing.

The position of your kiln is also important. See chapter 2 for specifics on siting a small, electric test kiln.

STUDIO VENTILATION

Proper ventilation isn't as easy to provide as you might think. Simply putting an exhaust fan in a window has a drawback: every cubic foot (28,317cc) of dusty air that you exhaust must be replaced by a cubic foot (28,317cc)

Opposite page: Lynda Curtis
Condah Series (detail). 1993
Each 3x6in (7.6x15.2cm)
PHOTOGRAPH BY BOBBY HANSSON

Right: Bernadette Stillo
Unite as One. 1993
5³⁄₄x7³⁄₄in
(14.6x19.7cm)
PHOTOGRAPH BY BOBBY HANSSON

of clean air. In the summer, you'll be hot unless that clean air is cooled, and in the winter you'll be cold unless it's pre-heated. Installing an air-conditioner won't work because an exhaust fan draws in replacement air quicker than an air conditioner can cool it. If you can't afford to ask an engineer to design a ventilation system for your space, place a three-speed exhaust fan, with a range of roughly 200 to 2000 cu. ft (5.66 to 56.6 cu. m) per minute (CFM), in an open window, and make sure that there's a window or door opposite to that window, one that can be opened when the fan is operating.

FIRE

Plan fire protection carefully. If you have a kiln, keep it well away from all combustible materials. Equip it with two shut-off mechanisms in case one fails. Even if you plan to do your firing elsewhere, keep suitable fire extinguishers on hand in your work space.

BODY PROTECTION

Wear infrared-blocking goggles when you look into a glowing kiln, asbestos-substitute gloves when handling hot objects, impact goggles when chipping, and a dust mask or respirator when appropriate. Make sure that the mask or respirator will do its job; a dust mask, for example, won't protect your lungs from gases or fumes. No mask or respirator will protect you from the by-products of a poorly ventilated kiln, so be sure that your kiln ventilation is good. And check with your doctor before using any mask or respirator. If you have asthma or a heart condition or if you're pregnant, a mask may do you more harm than good.

Keep broken skin from contact with clay or glazes. Apply a good emollient hand cream after washing your hands. If you have skin problems, wear surgical or plastic gloves while you work.

Avoid repetitive strain and lifting injuries. Make repetitive and/or forceful movements of the hands and arms in short bursts and take frequent breaks. Never work to the point of exhaustion or pain. Change positions frequently. When wedging clay, keep the wrists in a neutral or mid-joint position and use the weight of your body rather than just the muscles of the upper limbs. Maintain good posture, too. Store heavy bags of clay and other materials at heights that won't require you to bend your back when you lift. When you do lift something, keep your back straight and use the muscles in your legs.

For processes such as glaze-spraying and mixing powdered chemicals, be sure to provide local ventilation such as a spray booth.

Obtain *material safety data sheets* from your distributor, as well as mineral and chemical analyses on all the materials you use. Never use materials containing highly toxic ingredients such as lead and asbestos. Treat materials that contain over 1% free silica as toxic and provide ventilation and/or respiratory protection when using them. Make sure that you know which ingredients are toxic.

Always be prepared to provide your doctor with information about the chemicals you use as well as your work practices. Have a lung function test each time you have a physical examination. If you decide to use frits, glazes or other materials that contain lead, arrange for regular blood lead tests. Keep a well-stocked first-aid kit in your work area.

DISPOSAL

Dispose of all old clays and glazes and other waste materials in accordance with occupational and environmental protection regulations.

Bettina Elsner
Exotic Scene #1 –
Banana Tree with Monkey. 1988
34x34in (86.4x86.4cm)

Peter King and Marni Jaime
Palm Beach. 1993
126x78in (320x198.1cm)
PHOTOGRAPH BY GARY LANGHAMMER

Peter King and Marni Jaime
Mayan Relics. 1993
70x70in (177.8x177.8cm)
PHOTOGRAPH BY GARY LANGHAMMER

APPENDIX A

TEMPERATURE EQUIVALENTS FOR CONE-FIRING RANGES

ORTON STANDARD CONES

Cone No.	Bending Temp. Centigrade	Bending Temp. Fahrenheit
022	585	1085
021	595	1103
020	625	1157
019	630	1166
018	670	1238
017	720	1328
016	735	1355
015	770	1418
014	795	1463
013	825	1517
012	840	1544
011	875	1607
010	890	1634
09	930	1706
08	945	1733
07	975	1787
06	1005	1841
05	1030	1886
04	1050	1922
03	1080	1976
02	1095	2003
01	1110	2030
1	1125	2057
2	1135	2075
3	1145	2093
4	1165	2129
5	1180	2156
6	1190	2174
7	1210	2210
8	1225	2237
9	1250	2282
10	1260	2300

APPENDIX B

FLOW CHART OF TILE TECHNIQUES

MOIST CLAY
Rolling out slabs
Brush on slips and engobes
Impressing
Slip trailing
Direct carving
Pressing with open-face mould
Pressing with carved plaster block

LEATHERHARD CLAY
Brushing on slips and engobes
Incising
Inlay
Shellac resist
Underglazes
Sgraffito
Screenprinting with underglazes

BONE-DRY CLAY
Underglazes
Shellac resist
Sgraffito
Screenprinting with underglazes

BISCUIT-FIRED CLAY
Underglazes
Screenprinting with underglazes
Rubbing on stains
Sgraffito
Glazes

GLAZED CLAY
Overglazes
Lustres
Decals
Installation and grouting
Mounting

APPENDIX C

SLIP FORMULAS

All-temperature White Slip; 1922°F (1050°C) to 2300°F
(1260°C), Cone 04 to Cone 10
For Wet to Leatherhard Clay

Hexacil Ball Clay	.25.0%
Alkaline Leaden	.20.0%
Flint	.20.0%
China Clay	.12.5%
Molochite	.12.5%
Talc	. 5.0%
Zirconium Silicate	. 5.0%
	100.0%

To colour this white slip, add underglaze colours (judging proportions by eye) or commercial stains or oxides (1% to 15%).

Archie Bray Black Slip; 1922°F (1050°C), Cone 04
For Wet to Leatherhard Clay

Red Art Clay	.46.73%
Hexacil Ball Clay	.23.36%
Manganese Dioxide	.14.02%
Black Stain	.11.22%
Black Iron Oxide	. 4.67%
	100.0%

APPENDIX D

GLAZE FORMULAS

LOW-FIRE GLAZES

Waxy Satin Majolica
1922°F (1050°C), Cone 04; Oxidation

Ferro Frit 3124	.72.72%
Whiting	. 9.09%
Flint	. 4.55%
China Clay	. 4.55%
Zirconium Silicate	. 9.09%
	100.0%

A good, base-white glaze; breaks nicely over relief terracotta surface.

DeB's Squash
1922°F (1050°C), Cone 04; Oxidation

Flint	.42.0%
Colemanite	.38.0%
Lithium Carbonate	.10.0%
Nepheline Syenite	. 5.0%
China Clay	. 5.0%
	100.0%

Add:
Purple Iron Oxide	.10.0%

Nice yellow squash or mustard colour; breaks to maroon over terracotta.

MEDIUM-FIRE GLAZE

Toshika Green
2174°F (1190°C), Cone 06; Oxidation

Potash Feldspar	.34.5%
Whiting	.21.6%
China Clay	.13.0%
Cornish Stone	.17.2%
Zinc Oxide	.10.3%
Copper Carbonate	. 1.7%
Bentonite	. 1.7%
	100.0%

Semi-matt surface; breaks nicely over textured surface. Colour ranges from cool green to tan-, brown- and olive-green, depending on application.

HIGH-FIRE GLAZES

Charlie D. White
Stoneware 2300°F (1260°C), Cone 10; Reduction

Nepheline Syenite	.20.0%
F-4 Feldspar	.20.0%
Flint	.20.0%
Dolomite	.15.0%
Talc	.13.0%
Ball Clay	.10.0%
Whiting	. 2.0%
	100.0%

Add:
Zirconium Silicate	.10.0%
Bentonite	. 1.0%

Matt white in colour.

Lapis Blue
2300°F (1260°C), Cone 10; Reduction

Potash Feldspar	.40.0%
Whiting	.25.0%
Cornish Stone	.20.0%
China Clay	.15.0%
	100.0%

Add:
Bentonite	. 2.0%
Cobalt Carbonate	. 2.0%

Lapis-blue colour. Matt surface; breaks nicely to green and gun-metal grey. Must be applied very thinly, or it's just too blue.

APPENDICES

APPENDIX E

2300°F (1260°C), CONE 10 GLAZE REDUCTION FIRING

The general schedule that follows is for a 30 cu. ft (84 cu. m) natural-gas, updraught kiln, with a damper and flue on top of the chamber. The kiln has two forced-air gas burners with air blowers to control the fuel

- Load the kiln with your ware; the tiles should lie flat on the shelves and not touch each other. Arrange the kiln shelves at staggered heights so that there will be a free flow of heat throughout the interior.

- Position cone packs so that they're visible through the peepholes. This kiln does not have an automatic kiln-sitter shut-off. It does have a *pyrometer* (an electric temperature gauge), but the kiln must shut off manually when the appropriate cone has fallen.

- Start the kiln with both burners set on approximately ¼lb per sq. in (1723.5 Pa s). Set the pressure and blowers on 30%–50%. The gas-to-air mixture is adjusted to maintain a transparent blue oxidation flame. This is a low setting that will cause the temperature in the kiln to rise at a steady rate of about 150°F (83.3°C) per hour for about ten to twelve hours. For this reason, the firing is often started in the evening. Ten to twelve hours later, when you have to control the reduction process manually, it will be daytime.

- The next stage is known as *body reduction* and takes place at 1787°F (975°C), cone 07, for one hour. In firing terminology, reduction refers to the taking (reducing) of oxygen from the metal oxides in the clay body and the glaze, thus affecting chemical and colour changes in both. Body reduction should take place between 1733°F (945°C) cone 08, and 1841°F (1005°C) cone 06. When cone 07 is bending, adjust the burners to reduce the flow of oxygen into the kiln's interior. Adjust the airflow to the burners to its lowest setting. Increase the flow of gas to about 2lb per sq. in (13788 Pa s). Adjust and partly close the damper at the top of the kiln chamber to create enough back pressure to maintain a lick of flame on one of the lower peepholes. Care must be taken not to create so much

back pressure that it interferes with the operation of the burners. Partly block off the burner ports if necessary. For a period of one hour, adjust and readjust these controls every fifteen minutes; try to maintain an opaque orange flame from the burners. Back pressure should cause a slight flame to emerge from an opened peephole, but you don't want black smoke. You will also need to maintain the temperature and to control the flow of air within the kiln chamber so that reduction is uniform.

- To return the kiln's interior to a neutral atmosphere, readjust the burners and damper to achieve a neutral flame (multi-coloured, slightly purple, and translucent) that will effect a temperature rise of about 100°F (55.6°C) per hour. Maintain this temperature rise until 2237°F (1225°C), cone 8, about four to five hours.

- The glaze reduction stage is next. When cone 8 is down and cone 9 is bending, repeat the one-hour reduction process in the same manner as you did for the body reduction.

- Return to a neutral atmosphere. Readjust the burners so that the temperature rise is about 30°F to 50°F (16.7°C to 27.8°C) per hour. Continue for about two to four hours, up to 2300°F (1260°C) cone 10.

- When cone 10 is down, the firing is finished. Shut down the burners, and close the top damper. If you fail to shut the damper, the kiln will cool too rapidly, and your ware will probably crack. The cooling-down process will probably take twenty-four hours. Do not open the peepholes until the temperature is below 900°F (482°C). Do not open the door, even slightly, until the temperature is below 400°F (204°C). Remove the ware when it is cool to the touch.

Index to Artists and Photo Contributors

INDEX TO ARTISTS AND PHOTO CONTRIBUTORS

Opposite page: Frank Giorgini
Afro Tile. 1993
12x12in (30.5x30.5cm)
PHOTOGRAPH BY BOBBY HANSSON

Above: Frank Giorgini
Afro Tile. 1992
12x12in
(30.5x30.5cm)
PHOTOGRAPH BY BOBBY HANSSON

RESOURCES

To locate suppliers in the United Kingdom, look in the Yellow Pages telephone directory under 'Ceramic products and services' and 'Potters' materials and services' for pottery equipment and materials; 'Copying and duplicating services' and 'Screen printing' for screenprinting equipment and services. Advertisements in ceramics magazines are also a good resource.

ORGANIZATIONS AND SUPPLIERS
Bath Pottery Supplies, 2 Dorset Close, Bath BA2 3RF.
  Tel: 01225 337046
  General suppliers – materials, tools and machinery, mail order service.
British Ceramic Research Institute
  Queens Road, Penkhull, Stoke-on-Trent ST4 7QL
  Tel: 01782 45431
  Testing and consultancy service.
Craftsmen Potters Association of Great Britain
  William Blake House, Marshall Street, London W1V 1FD
  Tel: 0171 437 7605
  Ceramic Review – bi-monthly magazine.
  Newsletter – bi-monthly, with a readers' inquiry service.
  Shop for tools and books.
Pottery Crafts Ltd
  General suppliers – materials, tools and machinery
  Head office: Campbell Road, Stoke-on-Trent.
  Tel: 01782 745000
  Mail order service.
  2 Norbury Trading Estate, Craiguish Avenue, London SW16 4RW. Tel: 0181 679 7606
  Shop, mail order service.
Reward-Claygraze Ltd
  General suppliers – tools and machinery
  Head office: Units A & B, Brookhouse Industrial Estate, Cheadle, Stoke-on-Trent ST10 1PW. Tel: 01538 750052
  Mail order service.
  8–10 Ingate Place, London SW8 3NS
  Tel: 0181 720 0050
  Shop, showroom and mail order service.
  King's Yard Pottery, Talbot Road, Rickmansworth Herts WD3 1HW. Tel: 01923 720127
  Showroom, mail order service.

BOOKS ON POTTERY AND CERAMICS
Berendsen, A. *Tiles, a General History* (Faber & Faber, 1967)
Byers, I. *Raku* (Batsford, 1990)
Caiger-Smith, A. *Lustre Pottery* (Faber & Faber, 1985)
Colbeck, John. *Pottery Materials* (Batsford, 1988)
Colbeck, John. *The Techniques of Pottery* (Batsford, 1974)
Cooper & Lewenstein, Eds. *Clay and Glazes* (Craftsmen Potters Association of Great Britain, 1988)
Fournier, Robert. *Illustrated Dictionary of Practical Pottery* (A. & C. Black, 1973; 3rd edition 1992)
Fraser, H. *Glazes for the Craft Potter* (Pitman Publishing, 1973)
  Lynggaard, Finn. *Pottery: Raku Techniques* (Van Nostrand Reinhold, 1973)
Rhodes, Daniel. *Clay and Glazes for the Potter* (Chiltern Book Company, 1967)
Rhodes, Daniel. *Kilns: Design, Construction and Operation* (Chiltern Book Company, 1968)
Rhodes, Daniel. *Stoneware and Porcelain: The Art of High-fire Pottery* (Chiltern Book Company, 1967)
Riegger, H. *Raku, Art and Technique* (Studio Vista, 1970)
Shaw, K. *Science for Draft Potters and Enamellers* (David & Charles, 1972)
Sutherland, R. *Glazes from Natural Sources* (Batsford, 1987)
Wittig, Irene. *The Clay Canvas – Creative Painting on Functional Ceramics* (Chiltern Book Company, 1991)
Zakin, Richard. *Ceramics, Mastering the Craft* (A. & C. Black, 1990)

ACKNOWLEDGEMENTS

I would like to thank Joseph A. Taylor, president of the Tile Heritage Foundation, for having written the chapter entitled 'The Handcrafted Tradition in Tiles' and for having provided so many beautiful photographs to accompany it. His generosity and patience are as remarkable as the depth and breadth of his knowledge. Many thanks, also, to the following people, for their expertise and information.

  Lynda Curtis: Sgraffito (chapter 7)
  George F. Fishman: Mosaic assembly and installation (chapter 11)
  Richard Freudenberger: Giorgini Studio Tile Press (chapter 14)
  DeBorah Goletz: Kiln-firing schedules (chapters 8 and 10 and Appendix E)
  Renée Habert and Jim Stonebraker: Computer design (chapter 12)
  Sandra McLean and Robert Stratton: Screenprinting (chapter 7)
  Michael Spender: Tiles in Britain (chapter 1)
  Arnon Zadok: Installation (chapter 13)

I am deeply grateful to Bobby Hansson (Leaping Beaver Studios, Box 1100, Rising Sun, MD 21911), who has been photographing my work for years and who is responsible for the beautiful and dynamic photos that document the tile-making process in this book. His enthusiasm and expertise have been integral to this project. Don Osby, of Page 1 Publications in Hendersonville, NC, did a great job with the illustrations. My thanks also go to the skilled and enthusiastic tile makers who generously submitted photographs of their work and to the people listed below, who contributed additional photography.

  Chris Blanchett
  Tiles & Architectural Ceramics Books
  Fired Earth Tiles plc
  Twyford Mill, Oxford Road, Adderbury
  Banbury, Oxfordshire, OX17 3HP
  Nilüfer Alpsar, Kalebodur Seramik Sanayi A.S.
  Büyükdere Caddesi, P.K.: (P. Box) 154, 80620
  Levent-Istanbul, Turkey
  José Luis Porcar, Instituto de Promoción Cerámica
  Diputación Provincial, Plaza de las Aulas, 7,
  12001 Castellón, Spain

I am also indebted to my family, especially to my wife, Joyce, whose support and assistance were invaluable contributions to this project; to Gino Giorgini Sr., Jr., and III; to Sharon and Mitch at Jack D. Wolfe Co., Brooklyn, NY; to Dennis, Dot, and Mary at Northeast Ceramic Supply, Inc., Troy, NY; to the teachers, administrators, and students of Parsons School of Design, NY, who collectively make Parsons an environment for creativity in the ceramic arts; to Chris Rich, my editor, whose skill and good humour kept me on track and over the coals; to art director Kathleen Holmes, for her creativity and composure, and to publisher Rob Pulleyn, whose vision made it all happen.

METRIC CONVERSION CHARTS

LENGTHS

INCHES	CM	INCHES	CM
$1/8$	0.3	20	50.8
$1/4$	0.6	21	53.3
$3/8$	1.0	22	55.9
$1/2$	1.3	23	58.4
$5/8$	1.6	24	61.0
$3/4$	1.9	25	63.5
$7/8$	2.2	26	66.0
1	2.5	27	68.6
$1^1/4$	3.2	28	71.1
$1^1/2$	3.8	29	73.7
$1^3/4$	4.4	30	76.2
2	5.1	31	78.7
$2^1/2$	6.4	32	81.3
3	7.6	33	83.8
$3^1/2$	8.9	34	86.4
4	10.2	35	88.9
$4^1/2$	11.4	36	91.4
5	12.7	37	94.0
6	15.2	38	96.5
7	17.8	39	99.1
8	20.3	40	101.6
9	22.9	41	104.1
10	25.4	42	106.7
11	27.9	43	109.2
12	30.5	44	111.8
13	33.0	45	114.3
14	35.6	46	116.8
15	38.1	47	119.4
16	40.6	48	121.9
17	43.2	49	124.5
18	45.7	50	127.0
19	48.3		

VOLUMES

1 fluid ounce	29.6 ml
1 pint	.473 l
1 quart	.946 l
1 gallon	3.785 l

WEIGHT

0.035 oz	1 gram
1 oz	28.4 grams
1 lb	453.6 grams

TEMPERATURES

To convert Celsius to Fahrenheit, multiply by 9, divide by 5, and add 32.

To convert Fahrenheit to Celsius, subtract 32, multiply by 5, and divide by 9.

INDEX